A TEACHER'S INTRODUCTION
TO AFRICAN AMERICAN ENGLISH

A Teacher's Introduction to African American English

What a Writing Teacher Should Know

TERESA M. REDD
Howard University

KAREN SCHUSTER WEBB
Alliant International University

NCTE Teacher's Introduction Series

National Council of Teachers of English
1111 W. Kenyon Road, Urbana, Illinois 61801-1096

Staff Editor: Bonny Graham
Interior Design: Jenny Jensen Greenleaf
Cover Design: Barbara Yale-Read and Tom Jaczak

NCTE Stock Number: 50071

It is the policy of NCTE in its journals and other publications to provide a forum for the open discussion of ideas concerning the content and the teach-ing of English and the language arts. Publicity accorded to any particular point of view does not imply endorsement by the Executive Committee, the Board of Directors, or the membership at large, except in announcements of policy, where such endorsement is clearly specified.

Every effort has been made to provide current URLs and e-mail addresses, but because of the rapidly changing nature of the Web, some sites and ad-dresses may no longer be accessible.

Library of Congress Cataloging-in-Publication Data

Redd, Teresa M.
 A teacher's introduction to African American English : what a writing teacher should know / Teresa M. Redd, Karen Schuster Webb.
   p. cm. — (NCTE teacher's introduction series)
 Includes bibliographical references and index.
 ISBN 0-8141-5007-1 (pbk.)
 1. African Americans—Languages. 2. English language—Composition and exercises—Study and teaching—United States. 3. English language—Rhetoric—Study and teaching—United States. 4. English language—United States. 5. African Americans—Education 6. Black English. 7. Americanisms. I. Webb, Karen Schuster. II. Title. III. Series.
 PE3102 .N44R43 2005
 427' .089'96073—dc22

             2004025302

About the Teacher's Introduction Series

A Teacher's Introduction to African American English: What a Writing Teacher Should Know is the 6th in a series of books that speak directly to teachers of English and language arts at all levels. Ours is a wide-ranging discipline, and important scholarly developments in various aspects of our field can be highly complex, not to mention voluminous. We often wish we had the time to take courses or do extended personal reading in topics such as deconstruction, psycholinguistics, rhetorical theory, and the like. Realistically, each of us can read intensively and extensively only in those areas that are most closely related to our work. The Teacher's Introduction series, then, is geared toward the intellectually curious teacher who would like to get an initial glance into rich areas of scholarship in our discipline.

Three distinguishing characteristics of the Teacher's Introduction series make these books unique. First, targeting teachers across levels, the books are intended to provide easy access to crucial theoretical concepts and movements, but *not* to oversimplify. Thus, the books are in no way shortcuts to in-depth knowledge of any field. Rather, these straightforward treatments provide introductions to major ideas in the field and whet the appetite for further reading. Second, the books do not aim to "dumb down" complicated ideas, sanitizing them for an imagined "average reader." Many of the ideas are quite challenging, and we don't seek to patronize the reader by watering them down. Third, we don't want to send the message that every subject that is important to English and language arts teachers should be taught directly in the classroom. The Teacher's Introduction series books may not necessarily focus on classroom practice, but they will enable you, the classroom teacher, to add depth to your teaching.

The personal enrichment of the teacher is paramount here.

    We are grateful to Teresa M. Redd and Karen Schuster Webb for taking on the formidable work of writing so lucidly about the complexities of African American English.

CONTENTS

ACKNOWLEDGMENTS

We would like to express our deep appreciation to our colleagues at Howard University and Alliant International University who supported this project. We also would like to thank our NCTE editor, Zarina Hock, who believed in this project from the beginning and guided us so smoothly to the end. Finally, we are grateful for the legacy of the scholars who preceded us, the lessons our students have taught us, and the love our families have given us throughout this journey.

INTRODUCTION

On the first day of class, Jane Smith greets twenty under-graduates in her Composition 101 class at a small four-year private college in Bozeman, Montana. For the first time in her ten-year teaching career, she sees two African American students in the room, and she overhears them conversing in what she assumes is Black English. White, middle class, with little exposure to Black English outside the media, Smith wonders whether she is equipped to teach these students to write expository essays in Standard English.

Meanwhile, thousands of miles away in Newark, New Jersey, closeted in her office at an inner-city community college, an Asian American composition teacher mulls over a batch of diagnostic essays. Fresh out of graduate school and on her first teaching assignment, Kathy Wu does not know what to make of the profusion of errors in the papers before her. Since virtually all of her students are African American, she wonders whether Black English accounts for most of the errors she sees, and if so, how she should mark and grade the essays.

In an office down the hall, an African American instructor, Reggie Brown, is also troubled as he confers with a thirty-year-old woman who speaks and writes only Black English. He wishes he had taken a course in sociolinguistics. How should he discuss the student's use of Black English? How can he explain its impact on her writing?

These scenarios recur in composition courses across the United States. Again and again, teachers of writing confront what they see as the enigma of Black English, Ebonics, or what most linguists call African American English (AAE). The teachers' puzzlement reflects the national confusion about AAE—confusion that was all too evident in the wake of the Oakland [California] School Board's 1996 resolution on Ebonics. When the board declared

Ebonics the primary language of its African American students, the public furor that erupted revealed how little teachers as well as politicians and pundits knew about research on AAE.

Since the Oakland controversy, a number of linguists and educators have attempted to elucidate AAE for the public. But they have yet to specifically address the concerns of teachers of writing. These teachers need to understand not only what AAE is, but also what role it may play in students' mastery of Standard Written English (SWE), the standard for academic and professional writing. Writing teachers need a concise, coherent, and current source that introduces them to the major schools of thought—without polemics or unnecessary jargon—so that they can draw their own conclusions about AAE and understand how it might influence teaching and learning in their classrooms.

This volume seeks to fulfill these needs. It describes AAE and explores its significance for the teaching of writing by summarizing the best scholarship on AAE and applying theory to practice. Citing leading scholars in the field, the book answers the following questions:

1. What is AAE and how did it develop?
2. What are the distinctive features of AAE?
3. Does AAE affect students' ability to write SWE?
4. How can AAE speakers become effective SWE writers?

Chapter 1 plunges headfirst into the Ebonics debate. Page by page it explores whether AAE is "broken" English, slang, a dialect, or a language. These names matter because they convey messages about the status of AAE speakers inside and outside the classroom. Like the labels attached to AAE, theories about its origins also have educational implications, so Chapter 1 presents three competing theories about AAE's evolution. They range from the Eurocentric view that AAE evolved from the English of Irish settlers to the Afrocentric view that AAE imported features from the languages of enslaved Africans. In between we find the Creolist view, which describes AAE as an amalgam of features from English and West African languages.

Chapter 2 identifies the distinctive features of AAE: its vocabulary, pronunciation, grammar, and rhetoric. Many of these features can influence students' writing. After showing you how to identify AAE features in writing, the chapter refers you to Appendix A to practice with student writing samples.

Chapter 3 examines several hypotheses about the influence of AAE on students' ability to write Standard English. It first interrogates the claims that AAE is a sign of intellectual inferiority or an obstacle to learning SWE. Then it considers hypotheses that take into account language-learning strategies as well as the differences between speaking and writing. It also explores the role of the composing process as well as students' and teachers' attitudes toward nonstandard dialects.

Finally, Chapter 4 presents the pedagogical approaches that reflect these hypotheses, along with sample assignments (see Appendix B). Beginning with the traditional approach (which relies on grammar lessons, exercises, and revision), it proceeds to strategies designed to aid second language learners and to stimulate dialect awareness. The chapter concludes with a description of two other approaches that draw more heavily on AAE students' language and culture.

To help you apply what you are reading, the book provides five practical aids:

- ◆ Student writing samples with analyses of the AAE-related features
- ◆ Sample assignments illustrating each pedagogical approach discussed in the book
- ◆ Diagrams and tables to clarify concepts
- ◆ A glossary of essential linguistic terms (Throughout the book, glossed terms appear in boldface type.)
- ◆ A list of suggested readings for each chapter
- ◆ A list of recommended Web sites

Although this book will only introduce you to scholarship on AAE, after reading the chapters you should be better equipped to assist composition students who are AAE speakers. In other words, the book should help you diagnose, instruct, and assess.

Hopefully, the book will also motivate you to read more widely and more deeply about this important issue.

I

The Nature of AAE

Whether you realize it or not, your personal theories about the world guide your teaching. Therefore, if you wish to teach AAE speakers more effectively, you should examine those theories, especially your theories about language. In Part I of this volume, we invite you to do just that: to reexamine your theories through the prism of linguistic scholarship.

We urge you to read Part I carefully because some writing teachers have jumped to conclusions about AAE due to a lack of reliable or sufficient information. The extent of this problem was revealed in a survey conducted by the Language Policy Committee of the Conference on College Composition and Communication (CCCC). After collecting responses from nearly 1,000 college and secondary English teachers, the committee discovered that almost one-third of the teachers who responded had never enrolled in a course on language diversity (i.e., a course that would introduce them to AAE and other nonstandard varieties of English). Yet 96 percent agreed that such training was a necessity for anyone who was planning to be a teacher today (Richardson, "Race" 45, 54–55).

So what do writing teachers need to know about language diversity if their students speak AAE? Part I of this volume answers that question. Chapter 1 introduces you to AAE—what it is and where it came from—while Chapter 2 shows you how it looks and sounds. Chapter 2 does not, however, attempt to teach you to speak or write AAE; rather, it helps you *recognize* it when you see it in students' writing. At the same time, by surveying a wide range of views on what to call AAE, Chapter 1 prepares you to construct your own perspective—a perspective that will influence how you refer to AAE and how you relate to the students who speak it.

CHAPTER ONE

What Is AAE?

W hat's in a name? "Everything," says linguist Geneva Smitherman, "as we acknowledge that names are not merely words but concepts which suggest implications, values, history, and consequences beyond the word or 'mere' name itself" (*Talkin and Testifyin* 42). According to Smitherman and centuries-old African traditions (Asante 70; Nehusi 82–84), names wield power, and we can see their impact every day, especially in the composition classroom, where language commands so much attention. The language of our nurture often *names* us in U.S. society, with all of the positive or negative perceptions that are embedded within the name. Because of these perceptions, language, like ethnicity and social class, is a status predictor in the classroom, raising or lowering teachers' expectations and students' self-esteem. Therefore, what a teacher calls African American students' speech—and related features in their writing—is of no small significance.

Many African American students speak what we will call **African American English,** or **AAE,**[1] since that is currently the most widely accepted term among linguists.[2] Although all African Americans do not speak AAE, linguists estimate that it is spoken by 80 to 90 percent of African Americans (especially blue-collar workers and adolescents), at least among friends and relatives (Mufwene 32; Rickford, *AAVE* 323–24; Smitherman, *Talkin That Talk* 19). Occasionally, members of other racial and ethnic groups speak AAE as well; hence, they too are part of the AAE **speech community.**

You may have heard this type of speech referred to as Black English, African American Language, or Ebonics, among other names.[3] But it is the names people use to classify AAE that matter most in our classrooms. Historically, AAE has been labeled "broken" English, slang, a dialect, and a language. These names both reflect and affect the status of the speakers. Some names may lead teachers to view their African American students as lazy, illiterate, or even learning disabled, while other names invite teachers to see their students as multilingual learners. Likewise, certain names can make African American students feel ignorant or competent, ashamed or proud.

It is easy to imagine how the attitudes instilled by or embodied in these names might influence student performance in writing classes. Since teachers' and students' attitudes toward AAE *can* play an important role in writing instruction (see Chapter 4), this chapter aims to clarify what AAE is and is not. As we explain below, linguists agree that AAE is a dialect or a language rather than "broken" English or slang, but whether it is recognized as a language depends as much on politics as linguistics.

Is AAE "Broken" English?

Since enslaved Africans began speaking AAE, it has been regarded by some observers as **broken English,** "lazy English," or simply "bad English"—a fractured form of speech without logic or rules. After all, it appears to violate rule after rule of **Standard American English,** or what the American public calls **Standard English.** This is the variety of English privileged in U.S. academic, government, and professional circles as well as the mainstream media.

Despite its privileged status, the term *Standard English* is somewhat misleading, for there is no universal standard for speaking English in the United States. The spoken standard varies according to region (e.g., the South Atlantic versus New England). For simplicity's sake, however, we will refer to "Standard English" because these spoken varieties share many rules, especially grammatical ones. Moreover, there *is* a formal written standard, **Standard Written English** (**SWE**), which is "codified, prescriptive, and relatively homogeneous" (Wolfram and Schilling-Estes 281).

Whether the standard is spoken or written, AAE seems to defy the norm, especially the standard for formal writing. According to the rules of Standard Written English, AAE's verbs are missing or misused (e.g., *You the man* or *She be workin day and night*), its subjects and verbs disagree (e.g., *Mary get*), its words lack endings (e.g., *gettin*), and its sentences are poorly structured (e.g., *Don't nobody know what's goin down*).

Thus, over the centuries, Americans of all colors have characterized AAE as an incorrect form of English: even the African American poet Paul Laurence Dunbar, who made his name by writing verse in AAE, lamented in "The Poet," "But ah, the world it, turned to praise / A jingle in a broken tongue" (220). More recently, in 1996 when the Oakland School Board declared AAE the primary language of its African American students, critics such as former New York Mayor Edward Koch, CNN talk show host Bob Novak, and *Washington Post* columnist Mary McGrory characterized AAE as substandard English. And once again some African Americans joined the fray, including comedian Bill Cosby, who called AAE "Igno-Ebonics" (Gilyard, "It Ain't" 203; Vaughn-Cooke 139–52). Such epithets imply that AAE speakers are not educated or intelligent enough to learn Standard English—that is, that they do not know how to follow the rules of a language.

Yet linguistic research shows that AAE speakers *are* following rules, rules that simply differ from those of Standard English. Linguist John Rickford offers an instructive example of how rules govern AAE pronunciation. Arguing that AAE is "no more lazy English than Italian is lazy Latin," he explains:

> One reason people might regard Ebonics as "lazy English" is its tendency to omit consonants at the ends of words—especially if they come after another consonant, as in "tes(t)" and "han(d)." But if one were just being lazy or cussed, or both, why not also leave out the final consonant in a word like "pant"? This is not permitted in Ebonics; the "rules" of the dialect do not allow the deletion of the second consonant at the end of a word unless both consonants are either voiceless, as with "st," or voiced, as with "nd." (*AAVE* 323)

Ironically, the rule-governed nature of AAE was indirectly confirmed by some of the Ebonics parodies that proliferated in the media and on the Internet during the Oakland controversy. One striking example comes from a column penned by William Raspberry of the *Washington Post*. Attempting to ridicule AAE, Raspberry invents the following dialogue:

"What you be talkin' bout, my man?" he said, "I don't be offerin' you my grub; I be saying hello. You know, like, *what's up?*" (A27)

As Rickford and his journalist son Russell Rickford point out, however, this is not AAE, for it violates AAE's grammatical rules governing the use of the verb *be*. An authentic AAE version would read as follows:

"What you talkin' bout, my man?" he said. "I ain't offerin' you my grub; I'm sayin' hello. You know, like, *what's up?*" (208)

So Raspberry errs when he claims that AAE "has no right or wrong expressions, no consistent spellings or pronunciations, and no discernible rules" (A27). Indeed, as Rickford and Rickford observe, if AAE had no rules, how could AAE speakers understand one another? How could generation after generation of African American children learn AAE? (208). Clearly, AAE does have rules (as do all languages and dialects), and Chapter 2 introduces some of them.

Not only do the rules of AAE challenge the notion that it is "broken" English, but so does the very history of language. Drawing on that history in *Spreading the Word*, linguist John Mc-Whorter cites six additional reasons that AAE is not a substandard form of Standard English:

1. AAE is not derived from Standard English; it evolved from the English language alongside Standard English (7–8).

2. AAE is the product of the same sort of process that transformed Latin into French. Example: "[I]f the change from Latin *feminae id dedi* to French *je l'ai donné a la femme* was not a breach of Latin grammar, then how could the progression from *There's nobody here* to *Ain't nobody here* be a breach of English grammar?" (6).

3. AAE does not have "primitive" features. Example: AAE's omission of the verb *be* in *She my sister* or *He skinny* is the same sort of omission that occurs in the standard variety of many respected languages such as Russian, Arabic, Hungarian, Indonesian—even the original Hebrew of the Bible. (See *Atah ha-eesh* in 2 Samuel 12:7, which literally means "You the man," as in AAE's *You de man*.) (27–29).

4. Because we do not study AAE in school the way we study Standard English, most of us do not recognize the complexity of AAE, such as its rules governing *be* and pronunciation (10–11, 25).

5. Since AAE is not "frozen on the page" by printing and schooling, it has evolved further than Standard English, for instance, by simplifying sounds. Example: AAE simplifies the peculiar *th* sound in *them, these,* and *those,* producing *dem, dese,* and *dose* (25).

6. AAE is no more or less logical than Standard English or foreign languages. Example: AAE's double negative *I don't see nothin* mirrors the standard French *Je ne vois rien* ("I not see nothing"). In fact, the colloquial practice of dropping the first negative (*ne*) is considered "bad" French (26–67).

Is AAE Slang?

Instead of characterizing AAE as broken English, many Americans refer to AAE as **slang** or "street speech," that is, the lingo of the ghetto. Indeed, during the Oakland controversy, the Clinton administration and the *New York Times* classified AAE as such (Vaughn-Cooke 140). Unquestionably, AAE, like other varieties of English, encompasses a wealth of slang, words such as *chillin* ("relaxing"), *benjamins* ("$100 bills"), and *def* ("excellent") (Smitherman, *Black Talk* 65, 91, 105). From the Harlemese of the 1920s to the blues talk of the 1940s, from the Black Power chants of the 1960s to the rap of today's Hip-Hop, slang has remained one of AAE's most memorable contributions.

But AAE is much more than slang, for slang consists of short-lived, informal words coined and shared by a limited group, typically musicians, hustlers, or teenagers of a particular region or social class. AAE, on the other hand, includes words that have endured for decades, known primarily to African Americans regardless of age, gender, class, or region. For instance, surveys have documented that, unlike white Americans, a wide range of African Americans recognize AAE expressions such as *bougie* ("an elitist African American"), *cut your eyes* ("to give a contemptuous look"), and *ace boon coon* ("best friend") (Rickford and Rickford 93–94).

Moreover, any careful observer of African American life can see that AAE is not merely "ghettoese": it inhabits not only the inner-city streets but also most of the lower-, middle-, and even upper-class homes, churches, clubs, and other gathering places in African America. Therefore, to call a student's speech "street" or, in rural areas, "country" may associate the student with a lifestyle he or she does not embrace. Even referring to AAE as "slang" communicates a lack of respect for a tongue that the student's community considers good enough for church or home. Hence, linguist John Baugh found that many churchgoing AAE speakers took pains to distinguish "black street speech" from "the home language, which was devoid of 'foul language' or other 'bad words'" (*Beyond* 105).

But there is a more compelling reason why AAE is not slang: slang is simply vocabulary, and, as Rickford and Rickford remark, AAE is "much more than the sum of its words" (91). As we now explain, AAE possesses additional features—a distinctive pronunciation, grammar, and rhetoric.

Is AAE a Dialect?

Most linguists have classified AAE as a **dialect** since the 1960s, when they began to document the rules that govern its pronunciation and grammar. Dialects are variations of a language that are mutually intelligible but include some grammatical and/or pronunciation patterns that are unique to speakers in certain regions, social classes, or ethnic groups. Like other languages, English consists of dialects that possess distinctive features. Thus, even Standard American English is a dialect—just one member of the family of dialects that constitute the English language.[4] Yet much of the public wrongly assumes that the standard dialect *is* the English language because it is the dialect promoted by the people in power.

As our definition indicates, to qualify as a dialect of English, AAE must not only resemble other varieties of English but also vary systematically in distinctive ways. Many linguists argue that it does. For instance, linguist William Labov declares that AAE is "more different from standard English than any other dialect spoken in continental North America" ("Testimony"). According to Smitherman, the most distinctive grammatical difference between AAE and Standard English lies in the use of the verb *be* (*Talkin and Testifyin* 19). AAE speakers use "habitual *be*" to signal a recurring condition and "future *be*" to express future time.[5] On the other hand, they omit forms of *be* when the condition is fixed in time, unless it is essential for meaning, such as to indicate the past (*Talkin and Testifyin* 19–21). The sentences in Table 1.1 illustrate this complex grammatical pattern.

In the following scenario, Smitherman illustrates how the AAE usage of *be* can confuse teachers who do not understand it:

SCENE: First-grade classroom, Detroit

TEACHER: Where is Mary?

STUDENT: She not here.

TEACHER (exasperatedly): She is *never* here!

STUDENT: Yeah, she be here.

TEACHER: Where? You just said she wasn't here. (*Talkin That Talk* 25)

Chapter 2 summarizes other distinctive patterns of AAE, including pronunciation rules and rhetorical strategies that set AAE apart from Standard English.

Despite these striking differences, linguists such as Baugh, Labov, and McWhorter, as well as Wolfram, maintain that AAE is still a dialect of English because it shares most of the features of other American English dialects. That is why, they maintain, despite some baffling words, speakers of American English can usually understand AAE speakers. What these speakers say may sound different, but the underlying meaning (the **deep structure**)

TABLE 1.1. Contrasting Uses of *Be* in AAE

Feature	AAE	Standard English
Habitual *be*:	*He be busy.*	= *He is always busy.*
Future *be*:	*He be busy soon.*	= *He will be busy soon.*
Absent *be*:	*He busy.*	= *He is busy right now.*
Past *be*:	*He was busy.*	= *He was busy.*

remains the same. Although Smitherman has recently reevaluated this assumption, in her 1977 book *Talkin and Testifyin* she explains the concept well:

> [O]ne American English speaker might say, *John hit the ball.* Another might say, *The ball was hit by John.* In the deep structure of English, these two sentences are really the same; thus despite being expressed in different ways, their meaning is clear to speakers of English. Similarly, one [AAE] speaker might say, *He do know it.* And another [Standard English speaker] might say, *He does know it.* Again, both statements are the same in the deep structure, and the two different versions are simply two ways of saying the same thing. (193)

So similar is the vocabulary of AAE and Standard English that some linguists doubt those American English speakers who claim to misunderstand it. Pointing to the popularity of AAE in mainstream music, advertising, and media, linguist Anna Vaughn-Cooke declares, "There is abundant evidence that mainstream speakers not only understand Ebonics, they often borrow words and phrases from it, especially when these borrowings are economically and socially beneficial" (145). In turn, AAE speakers can readily understand media and print written in Standard English. To sum up, because AAE and Standard American English are so mutually intelligible, many linguists consider them both English dialects.

A number of linguists also argue on historical grounds that AAE is a dialect of English. Taking what is known as the **Eurocentric view of AAE,** they have proposed that AAE is a variety of English sharing far more features with British and American English dialects than with West African languages. Labov (*Language*), for example, as well as Walter Wolfram, Carolyn Temple Adger, and Donna Christian have compared many AAE features to Appalachian speech, which is spoken predominantly by southern white Americans. Meanwhile, other linguists have found that some AAE rules are consistent with older forms of American and British English, such as rules that substitute *was* for *were* and produce questions such as *Why I can't play?* (Poplack). These linguists maintain that such structures were already part of the colonial English spoken by the whites with whom enslaved Africans were forced to communicate, especially Irish indentured servants. Hence, Shana Poplack contends that "the grammatical core of contemporary AAVE developed from an English base, many of whose features have since disappeared from all but a select few varieties" (1).

Rickford, however, questions this Eurocentric view because some of AAE's most distinctive features (e.g., *he runnin, he be runnin, he BIN runnin*) are practically nonexistent in other varieties of English (*AAVE* 325). Moreover, he challenges the assumption that enslaved Africans readily learned the dialects of white colonists. Such an assumption, he insists, "requires a rosier view of their relationship than the historical record and contemporary evidence suggest" (*AAVE* 326).

Like the supporting evidence, the educational implications of the Eurocentric view are also not clear. On the one hand, if AAE is a dialect of English, the differences between AAE and Standard English may not be significant enough to account for most of the difficulties that AAE speakers have encountered in English classes. If so, we must look elsewhere for the major sources of their difficulties, such as pedagogical practices as well as teachers' attitudes toward AAE and toward the students who speak it. On the other hand, the similarity between AAE and Standard English may breed the sort of confusion that a Spanish-speaking student might experience while learning Portuguese. In fact, Wolfram and Schilling-Estes observe, "in some ways, it may be easier to work with language systems that are drastically different" (287). In other words, because many of the differences between AAE and Standard English are subtle, the differences may be difficult for AAE speakers to identify.

Is AAE a Language?

Although most linguists consider AAE a dialect, most would also admit that the distinction between a dialect and a language is not cut-and-dried. According to *A Dictionary of Linguistics and Phonetics*, dialects are "subdivisions of languages" (Crystal 114). So what is a **language**? Linguistic research has established that three rule-governed components identify a system of speech as a language: (1) pronunciation rules (**phonology**), (2) rules that convey meaning (**semantics**), and (3) grammatical rules (**syntax**). As we have seen, however, so-called dialects like AAE *also* possess rules for pronunciation, meaning, and grammar. That is why many linguists apply the test of mutual intelligibility to distinguish a dialect from a language: in other words, if speakers of African American English, Appalachian English, and Standard American English can understand one another fairly well, then theoretically all are speaking dialects of the English language.

Nonetheless, in the real world this test of mutual intelligibility has proven unreliable, as the Linguistic Society of America acknowledges in a resolution it passed during the Oakland controversy:

> The distinction between "languages" and "dialects" is usually made more on social and political grounds than on purely linguistic ones. For example, different varieties of Chinese are popularly regarded as "dialects," though their speakers cannot understand each other, but speakers of Swedish and Norwegian, which are regarded as separate "languages," generally understand each other.

Clearly, the classification of AAE as a dialect versus a language depends as much on politics as linguistics. As linguist Max Weinreich once quipped, a language is a dialect with an army behind it (Smitherman, *Talkin That Talk* 139). Considering that AAE speakers have historically occupied the least powerful positions in U.S. society, it is not surprising that, officially, AAE has not enjoyed the status of a full-fledged language.

Indeed, a growing number of African American scholars insist that the classification of AAE as a dialect rather than a language stems from racism—from the same institutional forces that tried to dehumanize Africans to justify exploiting them as slaves and as second-class citizens. Africologist Kimani Nehusi explains, "Since language is a distinguishing feature of humans, the denial of language is the same as the denial of humanity" (78).

In his criticism, Nehusi echoes linguist Ernie Smith, who has accused linguists of using a double standard to classify AAE. Smith claims that they have unjustly cited similarities in vocabulary to classify AAE as a dialect of English. If they applied the same criteria to English, he contends, English would be classified as a dialect of Latin or French. "It is universally accepted that English has borrowed the bulk of its lexicon from the Romance or Latin Language family," Smith states. "Yet English is not classified as being a Latin or Romance language but as a Germanic language" (52).

Since linguists cite similarities in grammar to prove that English is Germanic, Smith reasons that they ought to do the same to prove that AAE is a variety of English. But, he insists, they have not and cannot. They have not done so, he charges, because the weight of the evidence suggests that AAE has an "African grammar with English words" (55). To illustrate his point, he argues that AAE speakers do not "omit" a form of *be* in sentences such as *He busy*. They have simply retained an African sentence structure that can connect such words (*he* and *busy*) without a linking verb such as *be* (57). Nehusi cites other African continuities in AAE's verbs, adjectives, possessive case, vocabulary, tone, and intonation to demonstrate that, as enslaved Africans learned English, they molded it to fit the patterns of their West African (Niger-Congo) languages (111).

This **Afrocentric view of AAE**'s evolution is shared by scholars such as Aisha Blackshire-Belay, Clinton Crawford, and Charles Debose and Nicholas Faraclas. Since West African languages vary significantly, however, some linguists demand stronger evidence of an African structure for AAE (Rickford, *AAVE* 325). As an alternative, they offer a **Creolist view of AAE.** Creolists such as John Rickford (*AAVE*), John Holm, and Walter Edwards and Donald Winford agree that AAE evolved from a **pidgin** that fused English and West African languages. The most frequently cited evidence is the omission of the linking verb *be* (e.g., *They happy*), the absence of endings (e.g., *two boy*), and the simplification of consonant clusters (e.g., *them* = "dem"). All of these features have been traced to Africa through the Sea Islands' Gullah language of South Carolina (Stewart; Dillard; Jones-Jackson; Turner).

At this point, it would be logical to ask, "If AAE evolved from a pidgin, where did the pidgin come from?" A pidgin is not a native language for any speech community but rather a simplified language created for limited communication between two communities that speak different languages. Harris cites three conditions for the development of a pidgin:

1. Restricted access to the target language (in this case, English)

2. A shortage of bilingual speakers

3. The need to communicate

The history of slavery in the United States suggests that all three conditions were present. First, their enslavers limited the Africans' access to English. Second, although some enslaved Africans spoke more than one African language, only a select few had the opportunity to learn English well enough to serve as interpreters. Finally, although the need to communicate was forced, it was also a need to survive.

Over time a pidgin becomes the dominant language in a speech community. When this happens, the pidgin expands its vocabulary and grammar to serve the language needs of the community, and a **creole** is formed. This process takes place over many years, during which features from more than one language may shape the pidgin before a creole is born. The creole is then taught to the new generation as its language of nurture; thus arose Haitian Creole (from French and African roots) and Jamaican Creole (from British and African roots). In the African American context, AAE may have evolved from a local pidgin or from a creole imported by enslaved Africans from Jamaica, Barbados, or the slave trading forts of western Africa (Rickford, *AAVE* 327). Therefore, some creolists view AAE as a language that is distinct from English (Dillard; Turner).

Today Smitherman agrees that there is something "un-English" in the underlying structure of AAE grammar:

> [H]ow do you explain that there is a distinction in meaning between "The coffee cold" and "The coffee be cold"? The first statement means that the coffee is cold today, or right now, as we speak, but the second statement means that the coffee is cold on more than one occasion and perhaps most of the time. . . . [T]here are indeed deep-structure linguistic differences. (*Talkin That Talk* 15–16)

Smitherman also questions classifying AAE as a dialect on the basis of mutual intelligibility. She points out that sometimes listeners misunderstand AAE because they are not familiar with AAE communicative strategies, such as reversing the meaning of a word. As an example, she cites the "international diplomatic disaster" that occurred during the Cold War when boxing champion Muhammad Ali declared, "'There are two bad white men in the world, the Russian white man and the American white man. They are the two baddest men in the history of the world'" (*Talkin That Talk* 137). At that time, much of the white English-speaking world thought Ali was insulting the two leaders instead of implying, in the AAE tradition, that the men were powerful, tough, great.

Because of such differences, Smitherman has started speaking of the "language" rather than the "dialect" of African America. Recently, however, linguist Arthur Palacas proposed that the "mother tongue" of African America is *simultaneously* a dialect and a language. On the one hand, Palacas classifies AAE as a dialect of English because AAE and English are mutually intelligible, thanks to a large shared vocabulary and certain common grammatical features such as English word order (338). On the other hand, Palacas views AAE as a separate language when he looks at features that distinguish types of languages—for instance, whether a language requires its subjects and verbs to agree. He observes, "English and Ebonics are structured oppositely in many respects at their core—in the grammar of noun phrases and verb phrases and in the grammar of subject-verb agreement" (334). Even when AAE and English look alike, he notes, the similarity may stem from different grammatical rules. Both Standard English and AAE speakers might say, for example, "He is messed up," but the AAE speakers are unconsciously following a rule that also produces *You is messed up*. The rule differs dramatically from the Standard English rule that results in *You are messed up* (333).

If indeed AAE qualifies as a language, the educational implications could be far-reaching. As Smitherman observes, "[I]f we are dealing with a language, then the barriers reside not only in [teachers'] attitudes, but also in actual linguistic interferences that hamper communication" (*Talkin That Talk* 139). If such linguistic barriers exist, teachers may need the sort of linguistic training that an English as a Second Language program offers so that they can better assist AAE speakers in their classrooms. As for AAE speakers, Palacas contends that the discovery that AAE is a language may instill pride in them. After introducing AAE as much more than a dialect, he heard students who said in their own words, "'I always thought I was just stupid because of the way I talked; but now I realize that I'm bilingual'" (345).

Should We Even Ask?

While other linguists have been debating whether AAE is a dialect or a language, linguist Salikoko Mufwene has questioned whether linguists should presume to answer the question "What is AAE?" He suggests instead that they should pay attention to how AAE *speakers* classify their speech, and AAE speakers normally do so without identifying a certain number of distinctive features. Even when they do, AAE speakers tend to pay more attention to vocabulary and pronunciation than grammar (36). "[I]n many communities," Mufwene observes, "a language means no more than the particular way its members speak" (21). The preoccupation with whether AAE is a language or a dialect, he argues, stems from the stigma placed on AAE speakers (36). After all, he remarks, "we do not go around asking people to define or describe Cockney, Japanese, or Swahili for us . . . in order to determine what they are" (21). Thus, he concludes that there is no need to characterize AAE "otherwise than as 'English as it is spoken by or among African Americans'" (37).

Summary

Historically, AAE has been labeled broken English, slang, a dialect, and a language. These names both reflect and affect the status of AAE speakers. Linguistic research shows that AAE is neither broken English nor slang, for it possesses not only an enduring vocabulary but also its own rules for grammar and pronunciation. Linguists disagree, however, about its classification: While most agree that any classification will reflect politics as well as linguistics, those who consider AAE a dialect point to the similarities that make AAE and English mutually intelligible most of the time. On the other hand, those who call it a distinct language single out certain differences in grammar and communicative strategies. Finally, there are those who question whether linguists should attempt to classify it at all.

Whether AAE should be labeled as a dialect or a language also depends on a person's view of AAE's origins. Researchers of AAE do not possess the type of historical or written records they have for many European languages. Therefore, it has been more difficult for linguists to trace AAE's evolution. Whether Eurocentric, Afrocentric, or Creolist, however, all hypotheses acknowledge that AAE is different phonologically, syntactically, and semantically from Standard American English; it is the "why" that is debated, not whether there is a difference. The debate will continue as each hypothesis builds on new discoveries and as AAE continues to evolve.[6]

Notes

1. Terms in boldface type appear in the glossary, unless they are subheadings.
2. The term **African American Vernacular English** is also quite popular among linguists since the word **vernacular** (meaning "common everyday language") distinguishes it from the formal English spoken by many African Americans.
3. According to some scholars, these terms are not synonymous. For instance, the term **Black English** theoretically could encompass the languages of all English-speaking blacks, not just African Americans. Likewise, the term **Ebonics** was coined to embrace the multitude of languages spoken by people of African descent in the Caribbean as well as the United States (Williams vi). The terms also differ in terms of classification: *Black English,* for example, refers to a dialect of English, while *African American Language* suggests such speech is a language rather than a dialect.
4. Consequently, U.S. Standard Spoken English and Standard Written English are subdialects of Standard American English.
5. Lisa Green has observed that "habitual *be*" can also signal a perma-

nent property of a subject, as in *Some of them be big and some of them be small* (49).

6. Grammaticalization is the most recent hypothesis offered to explain the origin of AAE features. Through this process, the speech community invents grammatical items by using words in a variety of ways (Hopper and Traugott). The use, for example, of the innovative *had* with the past tense (Cukor-Avila and Bailey) produces "We *had* became real good friends" instead of the simple past, "We became good friends." This example represents a reanalysis of the Standard English past perfect. Proponents and critics alike, however, concede that much more research needs to be done to understand the nature of grammaticalization in AAE and the reasons for its occurrence.

Suggested Readings

McWhorter, John. *Spreading the Word: Language and Dialect in America*. Portsmouth, NH: Heinemann, 2000.

Mufwene, Salikoko S. "What Is African American English?" *Sociocultural and Historical Contexts of African American English*. Ed. Sonja L. Lanehart. Amsterdam: John Benjamins, 2001. 21–51.

Palacas, Arthur L. "Liberating American Ebonics from Euro-English." *College English* 63 (2001): 326–52.

Rickford, John R. "Suite for Ebony and Phonics." *African American Vernacular English: Features, Evolution, Educational Implications*. Oxford: Blackwell, 1999. 320–28.

Smith, Ernie. "What Is Black English? What Is Ebonics?" *The Real Ebonics Debate: Power, Language, and the Education of African-American Children*. Ed. Theresa Perry and Lisa Delpit. Boston: Beacon, 1998. 49–58.

Smitherman, Geneva. *Talkin and Testifyin: The Language of Black America*. 1977. Detroit: Wayne State UP, 1986.

Vaughn-Cooke, Anna F. "Lessons Learned from the Ebonics Controversy: Implications for Language Assessment." *Making the Connection: Language and Academic Achievement among African American Students*. Ed. Carolyn Temple Adger, Donna Christian, and Orlando L. Taylor. Washington, DC: Center for Applied Linguistics, 1999. 137–68.

Wolfram, Walter, and Natalie Schilling-Estes. *American English: Dialects and Variation*. Oxford: Blackwell, 1998.

What Are the Distinctive Features of AAE?

In spite of the controversy over its classification, linguists agree that AAE is a distinct and rule-governed variety of speech. What, then, are the features that distinguish it from Standard American English or other nonstandard American varieties such as Southern White American English? Wolfram and Schilling-Estes point out that in some instances a particular *aspect* of AAE pronunciation or grammar is unique rather than the feature itself, while in other instances the uniqueness is a matter of the frequency of use:

> For example, -s third person singular absence (e.g., *she walk*) is found in both African American and Anglo American vernaculars but . . . [s]ome African American speakers show levels of absence between 80 and 90 percent while comparable Anglo American speakers show a range of 5 to 15 percent absence. (171–72)

In addition to such differences, anthropologist Arthur Spears has demonstrated that AAE includes **camouflaged forms,** constructions that look like those in other varieties of English but possess unique uses or meanings in AAE (see "Black English" 850), as in *he come talkin bout gittin a job* and *he call himself workin,* both of which express indignation in AAE.

While certain aspects of AAE are unique, Wolfram and Schilling-Estes conclude that much of the uniqueness of AAE lies in its distinctive *combination* of features. Although the particular combination may vary from Connecticut to Mississippi to California to Texas to North Carolina or from rural to suburban to urban areas, there is a "basic core" of AAE features that crosses geographical boundaries (174–75). Some AAE speakers do not use all of these features or use them only some of the time, but nearly all African Americans understand them (Dandy 39).

In this chapter, we explore some of the distinctive features of AAE's vocabulary, pronunciation, grammar, and rhetoric, especially those that may surface in a student's writing. If you wish, you can practice identifying these features in the student writing samples in Appendix A.

Vocabulary

One unique set of features that is most recognizable and important is vocabulary. According to Smitherman, African Americans have forged a unique vocabulary from West African languages (e.g., *cola*), the traditional black church (e.g., *git the spirit*), black music (e.g., *funky*), and racial oppression (e.g., *the Man*) (*Black Talk* 17). As we stated in Chapter 1, these words include but are not limited to slang. AAE vocabulary can accommodate slang, historical words, novel meanings, and, at times, obscenity, just as Standard English does. The AAE speaker does not, however, have to use any of these words.

Slang

Typically coined by African American teenagers and musicians, AAE slang reflects the endless creativity of the African American people. Consider, for instance, such metaphorical terms as *hat up* ("leave"), *lame* ("out of step"), and *nickel n dime* ("petty") (Smitherman, *Black Talk* 159, 189, 210). Hip-Hop music in particular has generated some of the most noteworthy words. As anthropologist Marcyliena Morgan notes, today's Hip-Hop artists have transformed Standard English words in ingenious ways ("Nuthin'" 199):

- ◆ By changing the part of speech (e.g., the verb *fly* becomes the adjective *fly*, meaning "attractive")
- ◆ By turning prefixes into words (e.g., *dis-* from *disrespect* assumes the meaning of the whole word, as in *She dissed him*)

◆ By attaching suffixes (e.g., *converse* becomes *conversate* and *beautiful*, *beautifullest*).

AAE speakers also invent new slang terms by replacing words in a phrase. The phrase *get your groove on* ("get something going" as in dancing), for example, inspired *get my chill on* ("rest"), *get my grub on* ("eat"), and *get my praise on* ("worship") (Green 30–31).

But African American students are unlikely to incorporate such language in their high school and college essays: they recognize these words as slang and are mindful that most teachers frown on colloquialisms in academic writing. If they can switch to Standard English easily, they may even avoid using slang in class discussions. Therefore, writing teachers are most likely to encounter AAE slang during students' peer review group sessions and other types of collaborative learning activities, on electronic discussion boards and listservs, and in written dialogue, personal narratives, or creative writing.

To the typical American writing teacher, some of these slang words should sound familiar. As Smitherman has documented in her dictionary *Black Talk*, some African American slang has "crossed over" into mainstream English, enriching the vocabulary of the whole country (29). Long ago, when African Americans were concentrated in the South, AAE words of all kinds diffused into the speech of white southerners. Today, however, AAE slang in particular usually spreads via African American music to teens of all colors and then into mainstream newspapers and advertising (Rickford and Rickford 97–98). AAE sells everything from sneakers (e.g., *You the man* in a Nike ad) to vacations (e.g., *Chill out* in an airline ad) (Smitherman, *Black Talk* 29). Indeed, because of the influx of AAE words, celebrated writer James Baldwin once characterized AAE as "a language that permits the nation its only glimpse of reality, a language without which the nation would be even more *whipped* than it is." In a 1979 essay, he explains:

Now I do not know what white Americans would sound like if there had never been any black people in the United States, but they would not sound the way they sound. *Jazz*, for example, is a very specific sexual term, as in *jazz me, baby,* but white people purified it into the Jazz Age. *Sock it to me,* which means, roughly, the same thing, has been adopted by Nathaniel Hawthorne's descendants with no qualms or hesitations at all, along with *let it all hang out* and *right on!*

Although imitation is supposed to be the highest form of flattery, many African Americans resent this wholesale borrowing. Smitherman points out some of the cruel ironies of AAE crossovers:

> What is it about the language and culture of U.S. slave descendants, these outcasts on the margins of American life, that makes crossover so rampant, especially given the fact that the people who create the language and culture can't cross over. . . . Whatever the motivation for crossover, one thing is certain: in these postmodern times, there is a multibillion-dollar industry based on Black Language and Culture, while at the same time, there is continued underdevelopment and deterioration among the people who produce this language and culture. (*Black Talk* 30–33)

Given that so much African American slang is "out on loan to white people [w]ith no interest," it is not surprising that a new term replaces the old one in the African American community almost as soon as the old one is picked up by whites (Ralph Wiley qtd. in Smitherman, *Black Talk* 33; Smitherman, *Talkin and Testifyin* 70). For instance, Lisa Green found that *phat* ("extremely good-looking, tasty, or nice")—a term popularized by African Americans in the 1990s—was no longer in vogue with her African American college students by 1999, although it was still popular among her white students (27). Smitherman concludes that

> this dynamism is due, in part, to today's rather extreme cultural chauvinism among blacks, which says all whites are lames and if they are using this expression, it's gotten stale and unhip. . . . The other part of the explanation may be due to the historical inimical relations of blacks and whites which dictated the necessity for a black linguistic code. (*Talkin and Testifyin* 70)

Thus, teachers who try to keep up with their African American students' slang may find themselves on a fast-moving treadmill.

Says Clarence Major, author of *Juba to Jive: A Dictionary of African-American Slang,* "Black slang is a living, breathing form of expression that changes so quickly no researcher can keep up with it" (xxix).

Historically Black Words

In contrast to the ever-changing slang, the words that Rickford and Rickford call "historically black" extend across generational, geographical, and social boundaries in African America (94). Many of these words, such as *ashy* ("dry skin") and *suck teeth* ("to suck air through the teeth to express annoyance"), refer to characteristics of African American life, including cultural traditions, social distinctions, and physical appearance, yet many African Americans have no idea that other Americans may not understand the words (94–95). Hence, these are the AAE words that are most likely to surface in students' essays. We advise teachers, therefore, to have on hand Smitherman's *Black Talk* or Major's *Juba to Jive* for easy reference (see the suggested readings at the end of this chapter).

Novel Meanings

While teachers may encounter AAE words that do not exist in standard dictionaries, the most baffling words may prove to be familiar ones to which AAE has assigned a novel meaning. In AAE, for example, *kitchen* becomes the curly hair at the neckline, *fresh,* "excellent"; and *deep,* "serious." Sometimes the AAE term alters the standard meaning only slightly; hence, *wack,* meaning "incredibly deficient," is derived from *wacky,* defined in Standard English as "absurd or irrational" (Morgan, "Nuthin'" 198). At other times, the AAE term conveys the opposite of the standard meaning: it "flips the script." The classic example is *bad,* meaning "very good," but there are a host of others, such as *rags* ("stylish clothes") and *shut up* ("talk on") (Smitherman, *Black Talk* 241, 260). In addition, traditionally negative words sometimes assume positive connotations in AAE, among them *mean, stupid, dope,* and *phat,* all meaning "excellent." According to Spears, this type of **semantic inversion** is just one way in which AAE speakers exercise their broad sense of "semantic license," which entitles them to invent words as needed ("Directness" 248).

So-Called Obscenity

Perhaps the least understood AAE words are what most other Americans and even some African Americans consider obscenity. For instance, Smitherman discusses the notorious AAE term *muthafucka* (or *mutha* or *M.F.*). Although it can sting like a curse word (*That no-good muthafucka*), it can also express admiration (*He a bad muthafucka*) or add weight to a statement (*You muthafuckin right*) (*Talkin and Testifyin* 60). Some students may submit poems or post online messages that draw on this vocabulary—much to the shock and dismay of their teachers. If so, Spears urges us to keep in mind that many AAE speakers do not consider such terms obscene ("African-American" 242). Though he concedes that "obscenity, in the final analysis, is in the ears of the hearer," he argues that some "obscene" AAE words have been "neutralized" because they are "negative, positive, or neutral in force depending on how they are used" (232). In fact, sometimes an AAE speaker will employ such words merely for their rhythmic quality (237). This so-called obscenity illustrates what applies to most AAE vocabulary: to understand it, you must know the sociocultural frame of reference.

Pronunciation

At first glance, AAE pronunciation may not seem as relevant to writing instruction as vocabulary is. A writing teacher might assume that the pronunciation of AAE—the sounds of words and the intonation—rarely influences students' written work. Yet research suggests that AAE pronunciation can affect students' spelling as well as the comprehensibility of their speech (O'Neal and Trabasso 185; Gilyard, *Let's Flip* 69), especially when students are learning to read and write. Even college students may write what they hear other AAE speakers say: English professor Charles

Coleman has found instances of *stalk* for *stork, use to* for *used to, doggy dog world* for *dog eat dog world,* and other aural/oral misspellings in their academic writing (488–89). Spelling, though, is not the only relevant issue. AAE pronunciation deserves our attention because it can lead to gross educational injustices. As a result of AAE pronunciation, many AAE speakers have been placed in special education and speech therapy classes, or they have become the targets of discrimination (Bailey and Thomas 85). Thus, there are a number of reasons we should take a closer look at the AAE sound system.

In some ways, AAE speakers sound like southern white Americans. After all, both groups pronounce *I* as "Ah" and *pen* as "pin" (Rickford and Rickford 99). Such similarities, however, do not make AAE pronunciation any less distinctive. First of all, it is likely that in the South, where 90 percent of African Americans lived until the twentieth century, white families on plantations and tenant farms picked up these features from African Americans (Rickford and Rickford 100). Second, Bailey and Thomas have documented how changes in Southern White pronunciation since the mid-1800s have magnified the differences between Southern White and African American speech (106). Most important, AAE includes features of pronunciation that are not found in Southern White speech (Rickford and Rickford 100). Consequently, McWhorter remarks, "Most Americans, and especially black ones, can almost always tell that a person is black even on the phone, and even when the speaker is using standard English sentences" (*Word* 133).

So what makes AAE sound "black"? According to Smitherman, "the real distinctiveness—and beauty—in the black sound system lies in . . . its speech rhythms, voice inflections, and tonal patterns" (*Talkin and Testifyin* 17). For instance, AAE speakers sometimes vary vowels for emphasis (*Sang good now, y'all*) or adopt a lyrical tone (*I say Lo-rd, Lo-rd, Lo-rd*) (*Talkin and Testifyin* 18, 135). We explore these musical qualities when we turn to rhetorical strategies at the end of this chapter. Now, however, let us consider how AAE speakers articulate vowels and consonants and the syllables that contain them. As Rickford and Rickford explain, these pronunciations are "highly systematic, and not the careless or haphazard pronunciations that observers often mistake them for" (104). Just recall Rickford's example in Chapter 1: although AAE speakers omit the final consonant in *test* and *hand*, they retain the final consonant in *pant* because *pant* does not end with two **voiceless** consonants (such as *st*) or two **voiced** consonants (such as *nd*) (*AAVE* 323).

Syllables

AAE speakers may stress the first syllable of a word instead of the second ("PO-lice"). On the other hand, if a syllable is un-stressed, they may omit it, as in "fraid" (from *afraid*) or "sec't'ry" (from *secretary*) (Rickford, *AAVE* 5).

Vowels

In AAE, vowels may change substantially (Smitherman, *Talkin That Talk* 23–25; Rickford, *AAVE* 4–5), as illustrated below:

- ◆ *Ing/ink:* In words such as *thing* and *think*, *ing* sounds like "ang" and *ink* sounds like "ank," producing "thang" and "thank."

- ◆ *Complex vowels:* Complex vowel sounds (**diphthongs**) like those in the word *nice* are often simplified so that *nice* sounds like "nahs."

- ◆ *"E":* Before nasal sounds such as *m*, *n*, and *ng*, the vowel *e* sounds like *i*, making *pen* sound like "pin."

Consonants

AAE transforms consonants far more than vowels and in ways that resemble the sounds of West African languages (Smith 56). As the following list reveals, AAE tends to omit or simplify consonants, especially at the end of a word:

- ◆ *Th sounds:* pronunciation of initial *th* in a syllable as "d" or "v" (*them* = "dem," *brother* = "bruvver") and final *th* as "f" or "t" (*mouth* = "mouf")

- ◆ *R sound:* absence of *r* after a vowel (*more* = "mow")

- ◆ *L sound:* absence of middle and final *l* (*help* = "hep")

- *V and Z sounds:* pronunciation of *v* as "b" and *z* as "d" before a nasal sound (*seven* = "seben," *isn't* = "idn")

- *Str:* pronunciation of *str* as "skr" when *str* begins a syllable (*street* = "skreet")

- *Ing:* pronunciation of *ng* as "n" in multisyllabic words ending in *ing* (*walking* = "walkin")

- *Consonant clusters:* simplification of most consonant clusters at the end of a word (*test* = "tes")

- *Adjacent consonants:* transposition of adjacent consonants (*ask* = "aks") (Smitherman, *Talkin and Testifyin* 17; Rickford, *AAVE* 4–5)

AAE also contracts whole words; for example, *I don't know* becomes "I 'on know"; *and them,* "nem"; and *I am going to,* "I gon" or "Ima" (Rickford, *AAVE* 5, 7; Smitherman, *Talkin That Talk* 23–25, *Talkin and Testifyin* 17–18).

Spelling

From these pronunciation patterns, you can see how easy it is to confuse certain words from AAE and Standard English. As reading specialist Evelyn Dandy observes, AAE produces many words that are pronounced the same but spelled differently; for example, "den" could mean *den* or *then* and "coat" could mean *coat* or *court* (46). According to English professor Keith Gilyard, such AAE-related homophones account for some of the misspellings he sees in AAE speakers' papers, such as the misspelling of *mind* in *I really wouldn't mine having an Acura Legend* (*Let's Flip* 69). Therefore, to avoid misunderstandings, teachers must pay attention to the context of such words.

But what about the AAE words that are spelled the same yet pronounced differently? Hip-Hop artists have attempted to avoid writing homonyms by inventing spellings that reflect AAE's distinctive pronunciation and meanings. Morgan lists some Hip-Hop spelling rules:

Er: The *-er* ending on words with two or more syllables is spelled *-a, -uh,* or *-ah,* as in *brotha* ("brother").

Ing: The *-ing* ending is written as *-in* or *-un,* as in *sumthin* ("something") and *thumpun* ("thumping").

Reduced Words: Syllables are reduced and vowels assimilated so that "all right" is spelled *aight.* ("Nuthin'" 201–204)

Although such novel spellings may appear in students' creative and informal writing, they probably will not emerge in students' academic essays. In fact, AAE accounts for only a small proportion of AAE speakers' misspellings of Standard English words. In fact, in one experiment most African American children did not spell even AAE-related homophones the same as long as the words were presented in a sentence (O'Neal and Trabasso 179).

Grammar

Of all the features of AAE, grammar is the most distinctive for linguists and the most relevant for writing teachers. Compared to Standard American English, AAE relies less on word endings to convey grammatical information, boasts a more complex verb system, and accesses a wider range of sentence patterns.

Below, we look at the most striking characteristics of nouns, pronouns, adjectives, adverbs, verbs, and sentence patterns in AAE. As we examine these features, keep the following principles in mind:

1. AAE is "streamlined" (Palacas 340): just as Old English evolved into a language with fewer grammatical word endings, so has AAE, surpassing Standard American English (Gilyard, *Let's Flip* 68).

2. AAE can depend less on word endings because it depends more on contextual clues in the sentence or situation (Smitherman, *Talkin and Testifyin* 25).

3. In spite of its tendency toward streamlining, AAE retains a highly complex verb system that emphasizes *how* something happened rather than when it happened (Nehusi 93–94).

4. For many of the grammatical peculiarities of AAE, there are parallels in the languages that West Africans spoke before they

were enslaved (Nehusi 92–99; Smitherman, *Talkin and Testifyin* 55–57).

5. Many grammatical forms that look standard are camouflaged: they possess different meanings and uses (Spears, "Black English" 850).

6. Use of AAE grammar varies according to social class, gender, and age: African Americans who are working class, male, or young are more likely than others to use AAE grammar (Rickford and Rickford 126–27). An individual will, however, employ certain features of AAE grammar to varying degrees, depending on the particular sentence, audience, topic, or some other aspect of the situation. As Smitherman says, "[D]o not expect *all* Black English speakers to use *all* these patterns *all* the time" (*Talkin and Testifyin* 31). In short, like speakers of Standard English, AAE speakers exercise their "linguistic options" (Smitherman, *Talkin and Testifyin* 25).

7. In many ways, AAE is converging with Standard American English. Caught in this transitional stage, AAE speakers may alternate between AAE and standard forms in the same breath. Also, because African Americans were denied an adequate education for centuries, AAE speakers produce some **hypercorrections**, forms created as a result of overgeneralizing from standard rules (Smitherman, *Talkin and Testifyin* 28, 32).

8. AAE grammatical features are not errors; they simply conform to a different set of rules than Standard Written English does. In situations where the average reader would expect SWE, however, we use the term *SWE errors* to refer to all features (AAE or otherwise) that violate SWE rules.

With these principles in mind, let us turn to specific features of grammar. We have drawn most of our explanations and examples from Rickford's *African American Vernacular English* and Rickford and Rickford's *Spoken Soul*. Other sources are cited as needed.

Nouns and Pronouns

Both AAE nouns and pronouns exhibit the same tendency: to rely on contextual clues instead of word endings to indicate plurality or possession. According to linguist Lorenzo Turner (223–24, 227), anthropologist Ivan Van Sertima (140), and Nehusi

(92), this characteristic is typical of many African languages. Although AAE speakers normally add the plural -*s* to a noun to indicate "more than one," if another word in the sentence (e.g., *two*) already signals that the noun is plural, AAE speakers usually omit the -*s*, as in *two boy* (Rickford, *AAVE* 7). In contrast, Standard English is extremely redundant. As Dandy points out, the Standard English sentence *There are three books on the chair* "has indicated plural in three ways at once: *are*, *three*, and the -*s* on books" (48).

The presence of contextual clues also accounts for the AAE possessive. If a word such as *Jamal* precedes a noun (e.g., *house*), AAE speakers may assume that the juxtaposition of that word and the noun indicates who owns what. Hence: *Jamal house*. As Table 2.1 reveals, this practice extends to the pronouns *they* and *y'all* ("you all").

Do not assume, however, that all plural and possessive SWE errors are rooted in AAE grammar. Sometimes overgeneralizing from the standard rules for plurals and possessives leads AAE speakers to produce hypercorrections that have nothing to do with AAE's rules. For instance, AAE speakers may add the plural -*s* to nouns that have irregular plural forms, producing errors such as *mens* (Smitherman, *Talkin and Testifyin* 28). Other common plural and possessive SWE errors are simply a matter of spelling. Both AAE and non–AAE speakers may omit or mis-

TABLE **2.1.** Distinctive Plural and Possessive Features of AAE Nouns and Pronouns

Feature	AAE	Standard English
NOUNS		
Absence of plural -*s*	*two boy*	*two boys*
Absence of possessive -*s*	*Jamal house*	*Jamal's house*
PRONOUNS		
Additional plural forms	*y'all* *Tina an' em* (or *nem*)	*You* (plural) *Tina and her* *associates*
Absence of possessive form for *y'all* and *they*	*y'all ball* *they ball*	*your ball* *their ball*

place the apostrophe after a singular possessive noun (e.g., *a girls coat* or *a girls' coat*). Such SWE errors do not stem from AAE grammar since they reveal an underlying understanding of possession in Standard English. Unlike the AAE form *a girl coat* (which indicates possession through juxtaposition), these forms include an *-s* sound to indicate possession just as the standard form does (i.e., *a girl's coat*). The same sort of spelling mistake also turns up when students add the possessive *-'s* instead of *-s* to make a noun plural, producing phrases such as *five house's*. This too is not derived from AAE (which omits the *-s*) since the students clearly understand that they need to add an *s* sound to signal plurality.

Adverbs and Adjectives

Like nouns and pronouns, some adjectives and adverbs also lack grammatical endings. For instance, adverbs such as *sometimes* may omit the *-s* ending (Smitherman, *Talkin and Testifyin* 30), while past participles such as *concerned* that act like adjectives may omit the *-ed* ending in sentences such as *I am concern* (Smitherman, *That Talk* 170).

Verbs

The AAE verb system differs from Standard English in the way it indicates when something happened (i.e., **tense**) and how something happened (i.e., **aspect**). Let's consider tense first.

TIME OF ACTION

To convey the present tense in sentences where *is* and *are* function as **linking verbs,** AAE needs no verb at all. Instead of saying, "They are happy," AAE speakers can simply say, "They happy" (Rickford and Rickford 114–16). Meanwhile, to convey the past tense, AAE speakers can exercise a number of options in addition to using the standard past-tense forms. Like speakers of some West African languages (Van Sertima 141), they can rely on a contextual clue (*last night*) instead of a word ending (*-ed*) to signal the past, as in *I look for him last night*. Alternatively, they can use a lone past participle (*She seen him*). Or they can combine *had* and a past participle to indicate the past (*Then we had played*), especially while narrating (Rickford and Rickford 121–22; Green 91–92).

Linguistically speaking, the present and the past are the only tenses in Standard English, and the same applies to AAE. Therefore, like Standard English, AAE has no word endings to express future time. Instead, it employs unconjugated *be* (*He be here tomorrow*) or *gon* for "am/is/are going to" (*We gon win*). Or it uses *finna* (derived from *fixin' to*, a regional term) to refer to the immediate future (Rickford, *AAVE* 6). Table 2.2 summarizes these features.

MODE OF ACTION

Van Sertima found that West African languages "place more emphasis on the 'mode of action' than on the 'time of action'" (145). Like these African languages, AAE dedicates more of its resources to specifying how something happened than when it happened (Nehusi 93). Consequently, AAE offers speakers diverse ways to indicate that an action is in progress or has been completed. For instance, to refer to an action that is going on now, AAE omits the helping verb *be* before the *-ing* verb: *He*

TABLE **2.2.** Present, Past, and Future in AAE

Feature	AAE	Standard English
PRESENT		
Absence of *is* and *are*	*They happy.*	*They are happy.*
PAST		
Past participle	*She seen him yesterday.*	*She saw him yesterday.*
Verb stem	*I look for him last night.*	*I looked for him last night.*
Had	*Then we had played outside.*	*Then we played outside.*
FUTURE		
Unconjugated *be*	*He be here tomorrow.*	*He will be here tomorrow.*
Gon	We gon win.	We are going to win.
Finna (or *fitna*)	*He finna go.*	*He's about to go.*

talkin. But *be* reemerges in its unconjugated form if the action is habitual: *He be talkin.* On the other hand, if AAE speakers wish to emphasize how long the action continues, they can add *steady*: *He be steady talkin* (Rickford, *AAVE* 6). Compare these forms in Table 2.3.

If you think the progressive is complicated, take a look at the perfective. Although other English speakers may use a few of these forms, the range of perfective forms available to AAE speakers is astounding. As the following table illustrates, instead of combining a form of *have* with a past participle, AAE speakers can use unstressed *been* by itself (*He been sick*), the past tense after a form of *have* (*She had went*), or just the verb stem after a form of *have* (*They have work hard*) (Rickford, *AAVE* 6–7; Smitherman, *Talkin That Talk* 170). To indicate that the action was recently completed, AAE speakers need not include the word *recently.* Combining the helping verb *done* with a verb will do the job—and with extra emphasis: *He done finished it* or *He done finish it.* On the other hand, if the action was completed long ago, they can stress *been* (which we spell here as *BIN*): *He BIN finished* or *He BIN finish* (Rickford, *AAVE* 6).[1] Notice that when AAE speakers use *have, done,* and *BIN* as helping verbs, they often omit the *-ed* or *-en* ending on the following verb; in other words, they use only the verb stem. This occurs in the passive voice as well: *I am lock in my room* (Smitherman, *Talkin That Talk* 170). Table 2.4 summarizes what we've covered so far.

In addition to using standard helping verbs (e.g., *be* and *do*) in unconventional ways, AAE speakers have invented others such as *liketa* (meaning "nearly did") and *poseta* (short for "supposed to") while turning the verb *come* into a helping verb that expresses indignation (Rickford, *AAVE* 6–7). See Table 2.5.

Table 2.3. Alternative Progressive Forms in AAE

Feature	AAE	Standard English
Absence of *is* or *are* helping verb	*He talkin.*	*He is talking right now.*
Habitual *be* (or *bees*)	*He be talkin.* *Bees dat way.*	*He usually talks.* *That's the way it is.*
Steady as an intensifier	*He be steady talkin.*	*He keeps talking on and on.*

Overwhelmed? There's more, but we'll stop here. From the preceding analysis, it is easy to see why Toni Morrison once declared, "It's terrible to think that a child with five present tenses comes to school to be faced with books that are less than his own language" (qtd. in Rickford and Rickford 231). Although Morrison apparently counts the progressive forms as tenses, she vividly conveys the complexity of the AAE verb system.

SUBJECT-VERB AGREEMENT

Since AAE shuns endings for most verbs, it is not surprising that it does not require an -s ending to show that a verb takes a third-person singular subject in the present tense. Thus, in AAE, present-tense verbs are usually identical: *I walk, you walk, he walk, we*

TABLE 2.4. Alternative Perfective Forms in AAE

Feature	AAE	Standard English
Unstressed *been*	*He been sick.*	*He has been sick.*
Past tense after *have*	*She had went.*	*She had gone.*
Verb stem after *have*	*They have work hard.*	*They have worked hard.*
Done before *have*	*He done finish.*	*He has already finished.* (recent past)
Stressed *BIN*	*He BIN finish.*	*He finished long ago.*

TABLE 2.5. Unique AAE Helping Verbs

Feature	AAE	Standard English
Done	*She done finish.*	*She has already finished.* (recent past)
Stressed *BIN*	*She BIN finish.*	*She finished a long time ago.*
Liketa	*I liketa drown*	*I nearly drowned.*
Poseta	*You don't poseta do it that way.*	*You're not supposed to do it that way.*
Indignant *Come*	*He come walkin in here like he owned the place.*	*He had the nerve to walk in here as if he owned the place.*

walk, they walk. In contrast, Standard English is inconsistent. As Dandy points out, the third-person singular *-s* ending is "an irregularity, since no suffix is used to mark present tense with other persons" (50).

There are occasions, however, when AAE speakers use a verbal *-s* ending where Standard English does not, though the usage may vary regionally. If the verb is *be,* for example, many AAE speakers add an *-s* to mark the verbs for *you* and plural subjects. Thus, they will say, "you was" and "they is." They may also add a verbal *-s* for emphasis, as in *You know I wants to win* or *I loves my baby* (Pitts; Baugh, *Out* 127). Or they may attach an *-s* ending to indicate a recurring activity: *I gets my check on the first of the month* (Green 100–101; Smitherman *Talkin That Talk* 24). Table 2.6 includes these options. Notice that this table does not include all types of SWE subject-verb agreement errors. SWE errors in sentences such as *The cost of the books are too high* stem from the difficulty of finding the subject, not from AAE rules of agreement.

Sentence Patterns

So far we have focused on the structure of words. But the structure of some types of sentences also distinguishes AAE from Standard English. In particular, AAE constructs negative statements,

Table 2.6. Distinctive AAE Rules of Subject-Verb Agreement

Feature	AAE	Standard English
Absence of 3rd person singular present tense *-s*	*She walk.*	*She walks.*
Is and *was* with plural subjects and *you*	*They is some crazy folk.* *You was right.*	*They are some crazy folks.* *You were right.*
Emphatic *-s*	*I loves my baby.*	*I love my baby a lot.*
Habitual *-s*	*When I think about him, I gets excited.*	*When I think about him, I get excited.*
Narrative *-s*	*The man asked for some money. So I looks in my pocket. . . .*	*The man asked for some money. So I looked in my pocket. . . .*

questions, and sentences beginning with *There* and *Here* in different ways. Also, AAE sentence patterns are reflected in some of the constructions that writing teachers label as "mixed" or "fused" in students' papers.

NEGATIVE STATEMENTS

To negate statements, AAE speakers have retained the *ain't* of early British English but have expanded its use so that it represents not only *am not* but also *isn't, aren't, doesn't, don't, hasn't,* and *haven't*. So an AAE speaker can say not only *I ain't lyin* ("I am not lying") but also *He ain't never seen it* ("He hasn't ever seen it") or *He ain't got no further than third grade* ("He didn't get any further than third grade"). If AAE speakers use *ain't but*, however, they merely mean "only": *She ain't but six years old* (Rickford, *AAVE* 8; Rickford and Rickford 122–24).

Two of the preceding examples illustrate another noteworthy characteristic of AAE: double negatives. While AAE shares this trait with some other nonstandard English dialects, AAE boasts triple negatives, as in *I don't owe nobody nothing* ("I don't owe anybody anything"). Moreover, AAE speakers are free to invert the subject and helping verb to construct negative statements such as *Can't nobody beat us* (Rickford and Rickford 123). Table 2.7 presents all of these options.

TABLE 2.7. Negative Statements in AAE

Feature	AAE	Standard English
Ain't for *am not, isn't, aren't*	*I ain't lyin.*	*I am not lying.*
Ain't for *hasn't* and *haven't*	*He ain't seen her.*	*He hasn't seen her.*
Ain't for *doesn't* and *don't*	*She ain't got it.*	*She doesn't have it.*
Multiple negatives	*I don't owe nobody nothing.*	*I don't owe anybody anything.*
Inverted word order	*Can't nobody beat us.*	*Nobody can beat us.*

QUESTIONS

The negative inversion shown in Table 2.7 is not the only instance of AAE inversion that distinguishes AAE from Standard
English. AAE also inverts the subject and the helping verb in
indirect questions when Standard English retains the usual word
order and inserts *if* or *whether.* For instance, AAE produces *I
asked him could he come* instead of the standard version *I asked
him if he could come.* Ironically, while AAE prefers inverted word
order in indirect questions, it allows speakers to forgo inversion
in direct questions. Thus, instead of asking, "Why can't I play?,"
an AAE speaker may choose to ask, "Why I can't play?," as indicated in Table 2.8 (Rickford, *AAVE* 8).

THERE/HERE STATEMENTS

AAE offers speakers alternatives to structures such as *There is*
and *Here is.* Sometimes, AAE speakers substitute *it* for *there* in
sentences such as *It's a school across the street* or *It a school on
her street.* At other times, they substitute *they got* for *there are* as
in *They got some hungry women inside* (Rickford, *AAVE* 8–9).
They can also replace *there are* with *there go* to present something or someone: *There go my friends in the front row*
(Smitherman, *Talkin That Talk* 23). As Table 2.9 reveals, *here go*
operates in a similar fashion.

MIXED OR FUSED CONSTRUCTIONS

Many of the unconventional sentence structures that writing teachers see in AAE speakers' essays may be rooted in AAE grammar.

TABLE 2.8. Question Formation in AAE

Feature	AAE	Standard English
Inverted word order in indirect questions	*I asked him could he come.*	*I asked if he could come.*
No inversion in direct questions	*Why I can't play?*	*Why can't I play?*

Double Subjects and Verbs. Take, for instance, the so-called double subject. AAE speakers seem to repeat the subject in a sentence such as *That teacher, she mean.* Smith argues, however, that they are merely commenting on the topic (*that teacher*). Thus, as in some African languages, their sentence divides into a **topic** (everything before the verb) and **comment** (everything pertaining to the topic):

Topic	Comment
That teacher	she [is] mean.

. . . as opposed to the usual subject and predicate (57):

Subject	Predicate
That teacher	[is] mean.

This topic-comment structure may give rise not only to "double subjects" within one sentence but to fused sentences as well. Charles Coleman, for example, analyzes an example from a college student's paper, *There was this guy that came into the bank he was the banks mail man,* as follows:

Topic	Comment
There was this guy that came into the bank	he was the bank['s] mail man.

Says Coleman, "[T]he traditional explanation that these result from running two or more independent clauses together assumes

TABLE **2.9.** There/Here Statements in AAE

Feature	AAE	Standard English
It instead of *there*	*It's a school across the street.*	*There's a school across the street.*
They got instead of *there are*	*They got some hungry women inside.*	*There are some hungry women inside.*
There go instead of *there is* or *there are*	*There go my momma in the front row.*	*There is my momma in the front row.*
Here go instead of *here is* or *here are*	*Here go my picture.*	*Here is my picture.*

that students are working from a subject/predicate orienta-tion"(492). His analysis suggests otherwise.

In addition to so-called double subjects, Stefan Martin and Walt Wolfram have noticed what teachers might consider a "double verb," *tell say: They tell him say, "You better not go there"* (15). An observation by Van Sertima may apply here, how-ever. He points out that in the African American Gullah dialect of the Georgia Sea Islands, when the sound *sϵ* (pronounced al-most like "say") occurs "after a verb of saying, thinking or wish-ing," it "always means 'that.' This use of *sϵ* is common in some West African languages" (143). Thus, we might interpret the pre-ceding sentence as "They told him that he better not go there."

Object Complements. Martin and Wolfram have also observed an unusual sentence pattern involving the verb *call*. In Standard English, a sentence beginning with *They call themselves . . .* could be completed only with a noun phrase (e.g., *"The Wildcats"*) or an adjectival one (e.g., *poor*). But in AAE, in a pejorative state-ment a verb form can follow *call*, as in *They call themselves danc-ing*, which implies that they do not dance well (17).

Subordinating Conjunctions. Other linguists have noted the ab-sence of certain subordinating conjunctions in AAE speakers' speech and writing. Rickford points out the missing relative pro-noun subject *who* or *that* in a sentence such as *That's the man was here (AAVE* 8). Although Standard English often omits the relative pronouns *who* and *that*, it preserves them when the pro-nouns are subjects of relative clauses (e.g., *That's the man who was here*). According to Palacas, Standard English also preserves *that* more often than AAE does when *that* introduces noun clauses. Thus, the following sentence is more typical of AAE: *His reply was he thought the test was racist first of all* (330). Table 2.10 presents some of these distinctive sentence patterns.

In addition to constructions such as those listed in Table 2.10, Charles Coleman speculates that the frequency of what he calls "by strings" in his students' essays may be related to AAE. Cit-ing linguistic studies by Elizabeth Sommers and Francisca Sanchez, he suggests that AAE speakers use the preposition *by* in a more causative way than speakers of Standard English do. For instance,

Sommers recorded *Then she had a telephone call by one of her friends*, and Sanchez, *I got a black eye by this boy* (491). This usage, Coleman proposes, may account for sentences such as the following, quoted from a student's paper: *By making English the official language would take away one's constitutional rights* (490). The *by* phrase essentially becomes the cause of the action and therefore attempts to assume the subject position in the sentence.

Such constructions turn up from time to time in students' writing, but how often do students incorporate other features of AAE grammar in their academic essays? Not as often as you might think. After analyzing 2,764 essays written by African American seventeen-year-olds for the National Assessment of Educational Progress (NAEP) between 1969 and 1989, Smitherman and a team of independent raters found a "generally low" frequency of AAE grammatical features (*Talkin That Talk* 167). "Further," Smitherman reports, "certain prevalent [AAE] speech patterns occur very infrequently in writing, for example, the classic BE aspect, as in *They be tired*" (168). More recently, Elaine Richardson also reported a "low frequency and distribution of AAVE syntax" in the pretest and posttest essays of fifty-two African American first-year college students who had an AAE background (*African* 104–5).

TABLE 2.10. Distinctive AAE Sentence Patterns

Feature	AAE	Standard English
Double subjects	*My mother, she told me to go.*	*My mother told me to go.*
Double verbs *tell* and *say*	*They tell him say, "You better not go there."*	*They told him that he better not go there.*
Verb as object complement after *call*	*They call themselves dancing.*	*They don't dance well.*
Absence of subject relative pronoun *who, which, what,* or *that*	*That's the man was here.*	*That's the man who was here.*
Absence of *that* before noun clauses	*His reply was he thought the test was racist.*	*His reply was that he thought the test was racist.*

It is worth noting that Smitherman and her team concluded that the number of AAE grammatical features in essays from the NAEP had declined between 1969 and 1989 (*Talkin That Talk* 175). Nevertheless, given the popularity of Hip-Hop among today's African American youth, you might wonder whether Hip-Hop will reverse that trend. Certainly, we see a lot of AAE grammar at work in the Hip-Hop Nation. Smitherman explains why:

> Because many rap artists are college educated, and most are adept at code switching, they obviously could employ "standard English" in their rap lyrics. However, in their quest to "disturb the peace," they deliberately and consciously employ the "antilanguage" of the Black speech community. . . . [T]he use of the Black speech community's syntax covertly reinforces Black America's 400-year rejection of Euro-American cultural, racial—and linguistic—domination. (*Talkin That Talk* 274)

H. Samy Alim's research suggests that some African Americans flaunt AAE grammar not only to reject but also to connect. In other words, they consciously increase their use of AAE features whenever they want to "stay street"—i.e., to construct an identity that connects them to the young African American community (55).

Whether the frequency of AAE grammar is increasing or decreasing in school writing, one trend is clear: the incidence has remained high enough to generate public debate, a host of "minority remediation" programs, and a flood of new books about AAE.

Rhetoric

Compared to AAE grammar, **African American English rhetoric** is far more likely to surface in students' academic essays, especially in classrooms where most students are facile code-switchers, shifting as needed from AAE to Standard English. AAE rhetoric is the set of discourse strategies that represent how many African Americans *use* language. In most African American communities, the use of language is a high art; in other words, *how* and *why* you say something is as important as *what* you say.

Therefore, speaking is a verbal performance that can make or break your reputation (Dandy 74). According to Africologists such as Molefi Asante, Kimani Nehusi, and Jeffrey Woodyard, the African American preoccupation with verbal artistry is supremely African—the use of tone and pitch to convey varied meanings of the same word, the love of rhyme and wordplay, the storytelling theatrics of the griots, the rituals, the work songs.

Despite the recent publication of books such as Ronald Jackson and Elaine Richardson's *Understanding African American Rhetoric* and Richardson's *African American Literacies*, the classic source of information about AAE rhetoric for writing teachers remains Geneva Smitherman's *Talkin and Testifyin*; therefore, most of our categories and examples come from it. Smitherman's predecessors and successors, however, have also contributed significantly to our understanding of AAE discourse, so we add their insights as we present the strategies that give AAE so much "flava."

Discourse Strategies

Within AAE rhetoric, Smitherman identifies four primary discourse strategies: **call-response, signifyin, tonal semantics,** and **narrative sequencing,** to which we have added Spears's mode of **directness.** As you will see, these strategies unite the sacred and the secular experiences of African Americans—i.e., "church" and "street." At the same time, they synthesize opposites, such as ritual and improvisation (*Talkin and Testifyin* 103). Many also influence students' writing.

CALL-RESPONSE AND OTHER FIELD-DEPENDENT STRATEGIES

Smitherman defines *call-response* as "spontaneous verbal and non-verbal interaction between speaker and listener in which all of the speaker's statements ('calls') are punctuated by expressions ('responses') from the listener" (*Talkin and Testifyin* 104). A deep-rooted African practice, call-response has been best preserved in the traditional African American church, where the congregation punctuates the sermon with "Amen," "Say so," "Tell it," and the like (104). Whether engaged in a sermon or barbershop betting, the speaker and the listeners collaborate to create the discourse. According to Smitherman, call-response reflects the African worldview of the cosmos as "an interacting, interdependent, balanced force field" (108). It is, therefore, a **field-dependent** view that encourages writers to become involved with their readers by asking them questions, telling them to do something, or acknowledging them with the pronouns *you* or *we*.[2] "Field dependency is the hallmark of the Black style, a signature feature," declare composition specialists Gilyard and Richardson (46).

Smitherman's description reveals how dramatically the call-response strategy of AAE contrasts with the "objective" stance so often required in academic essays, where teachers normally expect writers to keep their distance by referring to readers via the third person (*one, he* or *she, they*). Not surprisingly, when Miriam Chaplin analyzed students' essays for the 1984 NAEP, she found that more black than white writers exhibited a field-dependent style, marked by a conversational tone and AAE culture-specific vocabulary (18). In a more recent study of college essays, however, Gilyard and Richardson discovered that essays with a field-dependent style tended to earn higher holistic scores from independent raters (45). Thus, in spite of the traditional exhortation to distance oneself from the reader, a field-dependent style may contribute to academic success by increasing readers' sense of involvement and thus heightening their interest in a text.

SIGNIFYIN AND OTHER FORMS OF INDIRECTION

Another defining characteristic of AAE rhetoric is known as signifyin. *Signifyin* (or *siggin*) is "the verbal art of insult in which a speaker humorously puts down, talks about, needles . . . the listener. . . . It is a culturally approved method of talking about somebody—usually through verbal indirection" (Smitherman, *Talkin and Testifyin* 118–19). Sometimes signifyin can be competitive and ritualistic, as in the notorious **Dozens,** a game in which one insults the listener's relative (typically "yo momma") instead of the listener (Smitherman, *Talkin That Talk* 276). At other times, it is more subtle, as in female "smart talk," when, for instance, a young man tells a stranger, "Mama, you sho is fine," but the woman replies, "That ain't no way to talk to your mother" (Troutman, "African" 222).

Signifyin does occur in school writing, though not as often as it might. Composition specialist Kermit Campbell suggests that AAE speakers' "signifying voices are muted, limited as they are by what they have been taught or perceive as appropriate for academic writing tasks" ("The *Signifying*"). Gilyard and Richardson, however, offer a skillful example of signifyin from a college writer who urges progressive African Americans to educate other Americans about false racial stereotypes: "By *enlightening the darkened* we will be threatening the 'secure' establishments America has created to prolong oppression" (46). Gilyard and Richardson explain that the student is signifyin because "the quality of light has been traditionally associated with 'knowledge,' 'goodness,' and hence White folks. Darkness has traditionally been associated with a 'state of ignorance,' or 'evil,' and consequently, Black folks. But here, the Blacks possess or will possess the qualities of knowledge and light" (46).

Such indirection plays a role in many types of African American discourse, not just signifyin. Morgan concludes that it is an essential tool for saving face, or "being cool," which is an important goal of discourse in both African and African American culture ("More" 252–53). Indirection, Rickford and Rickford note, was also a necessity for survival when enslaved Africans needed to communicate secretly right under the slavemaster's watchful eye. Thus, in the spiritual "Steal Away," they were not just yearning to escape to their heavenly home but anticipating a more earthly escape as well. This "language of double entendre" continues to serve African Americans who need a code that racist whites cannot understand (79).

Unfortunately, sometimes in academic writing indirection may lead to miscommunication. Consider the case of the first-year college student who wrote, "The cop that was driving yelled though the window and said, 'Yall don't have no business out here.' I thought who is he our father" (Troutman, "Whose" 31). A teacher might chide a student for indirection (as well as SWE errors), insisting, "Say what you mean" or "Get to the point." Yet most AAE speakers would appreciate the sly way that the student challenges the officer's right to tell her "crew" what to do (32).

DIRECTNESS

Sometimes AAE is not so subtle; sometimes even signifyin can be confrontational, or "in yo face." Because of their negative criticism and candor, such AAE speech acts represent the verbally aggressive discourse strategy that Spears calls "directness." According to Spears, directness embraces the following:

> cussin out (cursing directed to a particular addressee), playing the dozens (a game of ritual insults), snapping [brief insults], reading people (theatrically delivered negative criticism), verbally abusing people, . . . going off on someone (a sudden, often unexpected burst of negatively critical, vituperative speech), getting real (a fully candid appraisal of a person, situation, event, etc.), and trash talk (talk in competitive settings, notably athletic games, that is boastful and puts down opponents). ("Directness" 240)

Most writing teachers would find such directness inappropriate in academic writing. For instance, when teaching argumentation, they usually caution students against engaging in name-calling or other ad hominem attacks. Familiarity with AAE directness, however, is a starting point for helping students revise their strategies for academic audiences.

TONAL SEMANTICS

Whether they are uttering an insult or a compliment, AAE speakers may endow the statement with a lyrical quality that is unmistakably African American. As Smitherman remarks, in AAE "the sound of what is being said is just as important as 'sense'" (*Talkin and Testifyin* 135). The role of rhythm and inflection in AAE may have evolved from West African **tone languages,** in which tone conveys meaning (136). To convey meaning, AAE speakers employ a variety of musical strategies:

◆ *Talk-singing:* a combination of singing and talking (e.g., "Faaaa—ther, I-I-I-I-I stretch my hand, aha, to to—to— tooooooooo—to Thee")

◆ *Repetition and alliterative wordplay:* the repetition of key sounds, words, and sentence structures (e.g., "I am nobody talk-

ing to Somebody Who can help anybody" or "You don't catch
hell because you're a Baptist, and you don't catch hell because
you're a Methodist. You don't catch hell because you're a Demo-
crat or Republican. . . . You catch hell because you're a black
man")

◆ *Intonational contouring:* the manipulation of stress and pitch
to pronounce certain syllables in a more meaningful way (e.g.,
"There is a PUR-son here who is PO-sessed")

◆ *Rhyme:* rhyme in everyday speech, not just poetry and lyrics
(e.g., "In a revolution, you swinging, not singing"). (*Talkin and
Testifyin* 137–47)

Some African American students employ these musical devices, especially in informal writing (Ball, "Text" 279) or academic writing that targets an African American audience (Redd,
"Untapped" 236). For instance, in one experiment a student who
wrote "The Black family, knowledge, and values are the keys to
gain financial freedom" in an essay for a white audience wrote
"Education is the key, family is the key, values are the key to
economic stability in the black community" when addressing a
black audience (Redd, "Untapped" 236).

NARRATIVE SEQUENCING

In addition to their musical tradition, African Americans possess
a long and strong narrative tradition. Just as they may "make
music" in everyday speech, they may tell stories to explain, per-
suade, or impress. "This meandering away from the 'point,'"
Smitherman observes, "takes the listener on episodic journeys
and over tributary rhetorical routes, but like the flow of nature's
rivers and streams, it all eventually leads back to the source"
(*Talkin and Testifyin* 148). According to Smitherman, such narration normally takes one of the following forms:

◆ *Preaching and Testifying:* When traditional black ministers
preach, they normally dramatize the theme of their sermon using "gestures, movement, plot, real-life characterization, and
circumlocutory rhetorical flourishes" (150). Members of the congregation who **testify** (i.e., tell the truth) about God's goodness
also dramatize their experiences and visions (150).

◆ *Folk Stories:* Through the generations, African Americans have passed down countless stories, especially those about "underdog animals who outsmart their larger-sized enemies" (e.g., Brer Rabbit) and tricksters who duped their slavemasters (e.g., High John de Conquer). Says Smitherman, "all of these folk narrative forms have as their overriding theme the coping ability, strength, endurance, trickeration capacity, and power of black people" (156).

◆ *Tall Tales:* "Meant to be taken semiseriously," the tall tale, or lie, "is a contrived story about some unusual event or outstanding feat that usually has an element of truth in it—somewhere" (156).

◆ *Toasts:* Told in verse, the **toast** is a tribute to a "superbad, omnipotent black hustler, pimp, player, killer who is mean to the max" (e.g., Stagolee, Shine, Dolemite, and the Signifying Monkey) (157). For instance, "'Stagolee was so bad that the flies wouldn't even fly around his head in the summertime.'" (160).

◆ *Reporting:* Smitherman remarks that in AAE "the reporting of events is never simply objectively reported, but dramatically acted out and narrated," whether it is a rundown of the latest boxing match or a courtroom testimony (161).

Although AAE storytelling is vivid and concrete, it is not always appreciated. "Though highly applauded by blacks," Smitherman observes, "this narrative linguistic style is exasperating to whites who wish you'd be direct and hurry up and get to the point" (*Talkin and Testifyin* 148). Educational linguist Arnetha Ball has documented a preference for this circumlocutory narrative style among African American high school students, regardless of whether they were speaking or writing ("Cultural" 524). Dorothy Perry Thompson found similar evidence while investigating AAE speakers' performance on her university's writing proficiency test. For many of the students, the story they wanted to tell was most important; the abstract idea (the thesis) stated in the test prompt was not (235). Like the students in Ball's study, they meandered from one topic to another, weaving a web of loosely associated anecdotes.

Such a loosely structured narrative style runs counter to the thesis-driven, hierarchical method of organizing essays that is taught in most writing courses (Farr and Nardini 108; Heilker

78). Nevertheless, from her analysis of NAEP essays, Smitherman determined not only that the imaginative narrative task was the African American students' "strong suit," but also that the "narrativizing, dynamic quality" of African American rhetoric worked to their advantage in the persuasive tasks as well: essays with a "black discourse style" earned higher holistic and primary trait scores than other essays (*Talkin That Talk* 185). So let's take a closer look at these strategies.

Rhetorical Devices

To employ discourse strategies such as storytelling, AAE speakers draw on certain rhetorical devices, some of which Smitherman (*Talkin and Testifyin*) classifies as follows:

- *Exaggerated Language.* Known as **High Talk,** this exaggerated language features ornate diction and exceedingly formal syntax. Thus, Martin Luther King, Jr. declared a matter to be "incandescently clear," while a working-class African American man ironically asked, "My dear, would you care to dine with me tonight on some delectable red beans and rice?" (94).

- *Mimicry.* Occasionally, AAE speakers will imitate someone's voice, language, and gestures for greater effect. Thus, a woman complaining about her boyfriend remarks, "Like he come telling me this old mess bout [speaker shifts to restatin and imitatin] 'Well, baby, if you just give me a chance, Ima have it together pretty soon'" (95).

- *Proverbs.* Like Africans, African Americans are fond of quoting sayings to endow their speech with wisdom and power. These aphorisms include both age-old proverbs and current sayings, some religious ("My name is written on high"), some educational ("A hard head make a soft behind"), some racial ("The blacker the berry, the sweeter the juice") (95, 245).

- *Puns.* Smitherman notes that "punning in the black" demands an intimate knowledge of the Black Experience. She cites, as an example, a line by singer James Brown: "'I don't know Karate but I know Karazor'" (95–96). To understand the joke, she concludes, the audience must know that African Americans are reputed to be skillful wielders of knives and razors (95–96).

◆ *Spontaneity.* While AAE speakers often draw on formulaic structures (e.g., in toasts and the Dozens), they have to fill in the details. To do so, they must know how to seize the moment, as Malcolm X did when his audience expressed surprise at his admission that he had spent time in prison. Without missing a beat, he declared that *all* African Americans were imprisoned: "'That's what America means: prison'" (qtd. in Smitherman, *Talkin and Testifyin* 96).

◆ *Imagery.* Many AAE speakers are masters of metaphor and other types of visual language, especially down-to-earth imagery. For instance, an African American who disliked "wig-wearing females" exclaimed, "'They look like nine miles of bad road with a detour at the end'" (97).

◆ *Braggadocio.* While most whites consider braggarts show-offs, within the AAE community boasting is an acceptable way for speakers to exercise control and dazzle an audience. Thus, boxer Muhammad Ali, who dubbed himself "The Greatest," intimidated his opponent Sonny Liston and entertained his fans with boasts such as "'Yes, the crowd did not dream when they laid down their money, that they would see a total eclipse of the Sonny'" (147).

◆ *Style Shifting.* To Smitherman's list, we would add *style shifting*. As Richardson explains, "African Americans may consciously perform Whiteness or Blackness (by varying their speech patterns) to meet their needs. The function of these performances could be to create ethos, pathos, authenticity, distance, familiarity, irony, or for purposes of critique, to name a few" ("To Protect" 692). Sometimes, for example, AAE speakers exploit the differences between AAE and Standard English to make a point: an AAE speaker might boast, "'It's not simply that I am cool. I be cool. In fact, I been cool'" (Morgan "More" 265).

While many of these rhetorical devices can enhance writing, some are misunderstood within the Western rhetorical tradition that dominates the teaching of writing in this country. For instance, a teacher may admonish AAE speakers for using clichés, when in fact the students are summoning the wisdom of the community through proverbs or other sayings. Or a teacher may chide students for inserting a colloquialism when they are strategically style shifting to make a point.

A teacher may also censure a student's attempt to impress readers with a sermonic tone, big words, and fancy syntax when the formal language of academic discourse encourages some AAE speakers to model their prose after High Talk and the African American preaching style (Balester 78; Noonan-Wagner 6). On the one hand, this tactic can produce rhythmic wordplay such as "Affirmative Action is not giving handouts, it is giving a hand" and vivid imagery such as "It is a lot easier to focus on our Black youth because it is a lot easier to change the growth of a baby tree. . . . The old tree is set in its growth and will break if pressed upon too much" (Redd, "Untapped" 227, 236). On the other hand, the same tactic can produce grandiose diction such as "Continuing in my childhood growth, I began to want friends who would accompany me in my duty as a kid to communicate with adults" (Balester 88).

The formality of academic discourse may also inspire AAE speakers to use unconventional metaphors that may be misinterpreted. Gilyard and Richardson cite a striking example: a student wrote, ". . . then we will begin dealing with this deep seeded self-destruction and self-hate that has planted its poisons into the hearts and souls of our young adults. . . .'" (47). A teacher might assume that the student intended to write *deep-seated* when in fact the student had invented the metaphor *deep seeded* to symbolize how "this garden has been grown through the seeds of 'self-hate' and 'self-destruction' that have been planted in Black communities" (47).

Because of academic constraints and teachers' reactions, many AAE speakers are afraid to draw on their native rhetoric in school, even though its musicality, concrete imagery, and vivid storytelling can strengthen academic writing (Ball, "Text" 271; Redd, "Untapped" 236). As Charles Coleman has observed, some students completely lose their "voice," producing bland, vapid essays (495). Worst of all, many lose their childhood interest in playing with language.

Summary

This chapter shows that AAE possesses numerous features that distinguish it from Standard English and combine to make it a unique way of communicating. With remarkable inventiveness, AAE speakers have forged their own vocabulary, especially by endowing Standard English words with new pronunciations, new meanings, and sometimes new spellings. Meanwhile, they have created a grammar that is, on the one hand, more streamlined (as it requires fewer word endings) and, on the other hand, more context dependent and more "verbally" complex. In addition, they have developed rhetorical strategies that are interactive and narrative, direct and indirect, musical and visual.

Many of these characteristics, especially AAE rhetoric, emerge in AAE speakers' school writing. Yet AAE rhetoric appears to be "the neglected R." Too often writing teachers are so busy trying to eradicate AAE grammar that they fail to encourage AAE speakers to tap their rhetorical resources. While some aspects of AAE rhetoric conflict with Western academic rhetoric, AAE rhetoric has immortalized the likes of Frederick Douglass, Martin Luther King, Jr., and Malcolm X, and it has correlated with higher scores on writing tests. Clearly, it is worth nurturing.

Notes

1. Green identifies three types of *BIN* (54–60):

    a. BIN_{stat} (*a constant state*)
    He BIN running. (*He's been running for a long time.*)

    b. BIN_{hab} (*habitual*)
    That's where I BIN putting my glasses. (*That's where I started putting my glasses some time ago and I still put them there.*)

    c. BIN_{comp} (*ended a long time ago*)
    Yeah, I BIN called her. (*Yes, I called her a long time ago.*)

2. For some readers, the term *field dependent* may have negative connotations since field independence has been associated with higher achievement on classroom and standardized second language tests (e.g., Chapelle and Roberts; Hansen and Stansfield). The correlation may be an artifact of the tests, however, since they normally focus on control of language forms rather than on the field-dependent student's forte: interpersonal communication skills (H. D. Brown).

Suggested Readings

Abrahams, Roger D. *Talking Black*. Rowley, MA: Newbury House, 1976.

Alexander, Clara Franklin. "Black English Dialect and the Classroom Teacher." *Tapping Potential: English and Language Arts for the Black Learner*. Ed. Charlotte K. Brooks. Urbana, IL: National Council of Teachers of English, 1985. 20–29.

Balester, Valerie M. *Cultural Divide: A Study of African-American College Writers*. Portsmouth, NH: Boynton/Cook, 1993.

Ball, Arnetha. "Text Design Patterns in the Writing of Urban African American Students: Teaching to the Cultural Strengths of Students in Multicultural Settings." *Urban Education* 30 (1995): 253–89.

Dandy, Evelyn Baker. *Black Communications: Breaking Down the Barriers*. Chicago: African American Images, 1991.

Gilyard, Keith. "One More Time for Professor Nuruddin." *Let's Flip the Script: An African American Discourse on Language, Literature, and Learning*. Detroit: Wayne State UP, 1996. 63–71.

Heath, Shirley Brice. *Ways with Words: Language, Life, and Work in Communities and Classrooms*. Cambridge: Cambridge UP, 1983.

Jackson, Ronald L. II, and Elaine B. Richardson, eds. *Understanding African American Rhetoric: Classical Origins to Contemporary Innovations*. New York: Routledge, 2003.

Kochman, Thomas, ed. *Rappin' and Stylin' Out: Communication in Urban Black America*. Urbana: U of Illinois P, 1972.

Major, Clarence, ed. *Juba to Jive: A Dictionary of African-American Slang*. New York: Penguin, 1994.

Mitchell-Kernan, Claudia. *Language Behavior in a Black Urban Community*. Monograph of the Language-Behavior Laboratory, No. 2. Berkeley: University of California, 1971.

Richardson, Elaine. *African American Literacies*. London: Routledge, 2003.

Rickford, John Russell, and Russell John Rickford. *Spoken Soul: The Story of Black English*. New York: John Wiley, 2000.

Smitherman, Geneva. *Black Talk: Words and Phrases from the Hood to the Amen Corner*. Rev. ed. Boston: Houghton Mifflin, 2000.

————. *Talkin and Testifyin: The Language of Black America.* 1977. Detroit: Wayne State UP, 1986.

Taylor, Hanni U. *Standard English, Black English, and Bidialectalism: A Controversy.* New York: P. Lang, 1989.

II

AAE and the Teaching of Writing

Part I of this volume elucidates African American English—its classification, its origins, its features. But for teachers of writing, identifying AAE features in students' writing will not suffice. While familiarity with AAE can help teachers diagnose, ultimately they must also instruct and assess, and in the United States the standard for writing instruction and assessment is not African American, but Standard Written English. Thus, having identified AAE features in a student's paper, writing teachers must determine how to strengthen the student's control of SWE. To achieve that goal, they must understand what role, if any, AAE plays in the acquisition of SWE. Then they can decide what role, if any, AAE should play in the curriculum or classroom.

As writing teachers have wrestled with these issues, many have found themselves in one of the three camps that Gilyard calls eradicationist, pluralist, and bidialectalist (*Let's Flip* 70–71). Believing that AAE is a deficiency or an obstacle to learning SWE, the **eradicationists** ban AAE from the curriculum and classroom and seek to "drill" it out of students, often through grammar exercises. On the other hand, **pluralists** aim to reform *society*, rather than the students, so that society will accept AAE and SWE as linguistic equals inside and outside the classroom. Finally, although they agree with the pluralists' claim that AAE is not linguistically inferior, the **bidialectalists** stress that SWE is a prerequisite for success in academic and professional settings. Therefore, they teach students to switch from AAE to SWE to suit the occasion.

To help you develop your own approach, Chapter 4 introduces you to a range of strategies for teaching AAE speakers SWE. Before assessing the strategies in Chapter 4, however, you should understand the theories that spawned them. Thus, Chapter 3 explores psychological and linguistic theories about the roles that AAE and other factors play in learning SWE. Although recent research has discredited some of these theories, we still include them, for they persist in the minds of many teachers, shaping what transpires in the curriculum and the classroom.

CHAPTER THREE

Does AAE Affect Students' Ability to Write SWE?

Even teachers who regard African American English as rich and rule governed may wonder whether it hinders the mastery of Standard Written English. After all, the performance of African Americans on national writing tests has been disturbing. During the most recent national writing assessment, only 8 percent of African American twelfth graders produced "proficient" writing, while 41 percent scored below "basic" (Persky, Daane, and Jin). In the past, a high rate of SWE errors has contributed to the students' weak performance, with African American eleventh graders averaging 27 percent more errors per 100 words than white students (Campbell, Reese, O'Sullivan, and Dossey 219). At the college level, these statistics are reflected in the disproportionate placement of African American students in remedial writing classes (Lewis and Farris; McNenny and Fitzgerald).

Statistically, why have African American students' scores lagged behind those of white students? Some scholars have argued that the tests are culturally biased (see Chapter 4). Others have blamed the teachers. But because so many African Americans speak AAE, it is easy to implicate AAE. And for years, the eradicationists have done just that. Armed with statistics and stereotypes, they have sought to eradicate AAE in the classroom because they believe AAE hinders students' ability to write Standard English or to think abstractly.

Does AAE Limit a Writer's Thinking?

Eradicationists who believe that AAE is "broken" English are most likely to consider AAE a sign of limited thinking. For instance, if an African American student says, "Six cow," they assume that the student has no concept of plurality; or if another student says, "Yesterday he look," they assume that the student has no concept of time (CCCC 9). Although the linguistic evidence in Chapter 2 refutes these assumptions, eradicationists have found plenty of support from **cognitive deficit theories.**

The Genetic Deficit Hypothesis

First came the genetic deficit hypothesis. In 1969, basing his claim in part on misconceptions about AAE, psychologist Arthur Jensen maintained that blacks were intellectually inferior to whites. Of course, his claim was not new; for years such claims had propped up the institution of American slavery. What was new was the set of IQ tests Jensen developed to justify his claim. As a result of these tests, he credited white middle-class children with Level II intelligence (the ability to form abstract concepts) and black lower-class children with only Level I intelligence (the ability to learn through association). Jensen's work seemed to confirm the eradicationists' point—that blacks lacked the intelligence to produce a "fully formed" and "logical" language like Standard English.

Linguists, however, have exposed the fallacies in Jensen's argument. For instance, in 1972 the Linguistic Society of America endorsed the "Resolution in Response to Arthur Jensen." This resolution attacked the notion that AAE or any language was a sign of primitive intelligence. Calling nonstandard varieties "fully formed languages with all of the grammatical structure necessary for logical thought," the resolution states:

> Linguists have not yet discovered any speech community with a native language that can be described as conceptually or logically primitive, inadequate or deficient. . . . The minimal ability to learn and to speak any human language includes native skills of much higher order of magnitude than those used in the laboratory tests offered in evidence for Dr. Jensen's views. (Kroch and Labov 17–18)

The resolution also calls into question Jensen's methodology. Specifically, the resolution points out that "human intelligence is not

yet understood or well-measured by any current testing proce-
dure" and that tests that predict school achievement "should not
be interpreted as measures of intelligence" (Kroch and Labov 18).

The Verbal Deficit Hypothesis

In spite of the resolution, Jensen's views live on in publications
such as *The Bell Curve: Intelligence and Class Structure in American Life* (1994) by Richard J. Herrnstein and Charles Murray.
Thomas Farrell even revived some of Jensen's ideas in the pages
of *College Composition and Communication* in 1983. In his article "IQ and Standard English," Farrell endorses Jensen's IQ tests
as "valid and reliable" but rejects Jensen's genetic hypothesis
(471). Instead, he hypothesizes that African Americans who speak
only AAE cannot think abstractly because they are rarely exposed to certain grammatical features he attributes to SWE but
not to AAE. He explains, "The development of abstract thinking
depends on learning (1) the full standard deployment of the verb
"to be" and (2) embedded modification and (3) subordination"
(481). He even suggests that abstract thinking began with the
ancient Greeks (481).

    As Baugh points out, Farrell overlooks considerable evidence
that humans could think abstractly long before the Greeks took
up the pen (*Out* 12). Nevertheless, Farrell was taken seriously
enough to win a spot in a peer-reviewed academic journal. In
fact, since the 1960s, Farrell's hypothesis has been one of many
verbal deficit hypotheses that have captured scholars' attention.
Among the most influential verbal deficit theorists are psychologists Martin Deutsch (Deutsch, Katz, and Jensen) and Carl Bereiter
who, in the 1960s, proposed that lower-class black children per-
formed below the national norm because they grew up in "verbally impoverished" homes: it was assumed that their parents
rarely conversed with them, and when their parents did, the children rarely heard well-formed sentences. When the psychologists
interviewed these children, the children often failed to complete
sentences, name everyday objects, or express certain concepts and
logical thoughts. As a result, Bereiter concluded, "The language
of culturally deprived children . . . is not merely an underdevel-
oped version of Standard English, but is a basically non-logical

mode of expressive behavior" (Beireiter and Engelmann qtd. in Labov, "Academic").

Like Jensen's and Farrell's hypotheses, however, the verbal deprivation hypothesis has been refuted. As Chapter 2 of this book documents, AAE speakers grow up in a verbally *enriched* environment, an environment in which words are power and talk is art. Moreover, in his rebuttal "Academic Ignorance and Black Intelligence," Labov demonstrates that the verbal deprivation theorists' interview techniques produced spurious results. First, he records how a black child responds to a white man in a formal interview: the child seems "monosyllabic, inept, ignorant, bumbling." Then, Labov reports how the same child responds when a black man interviews the child and a playmate in an informal situation: "The monosyllabic speaker who had nothing to say about anything and could not remember what he did yesterday has disappeared. Instead, we have two boys who have so much to say that they keep interrupting each other." Apparently, the verbal deprivation theorists did not realize how much the social situation shapes verbal behavior.

Although there is insufficient evidence to support cognitive deficit theories, we continue to see their impact. We see them in the overdiagnosis of African American children as speech impaired and the overrepresentation of African Americans in special education classes (Green 227). In a vicious cycle, these statistics feed the deficit theories that spawned them.

Does Speaking AAE Interfere with Writing SWE?

Today many teachers reject the cognitive deficit theories but still assume that AAE interferes with the mastery of Standard Written English. These teachers include not only eradicationists but also those who believe that AAE is acceptable as long as students leave it at home. Such teachers notice that a student who says "my girlfriend house" omits the -'s while writing or that another who says "He walk to school every day" omits the -s ending on paper as well. To these teachers, it is obvious that AAE prevents those students from writing the standard forms. In other words, the teachers conclude, "You can't write right if you don't talk right."

The Dialect Interference Hypothesis

The teachers' conclusion echoes the admonitions of the elocution movement that dominated U.S. writing instruction in the eighteenth and nineteenth centuries. Consequently, the notion of **dialect interference** was hardly new when the term entered composition theory in the 1960s. At that time, *dialect interference* was a buzzword among reading theorists who had observed that many AAE speakers sounded as if they were reading AAE when they read aloud a Standard English text. Even earlier, theorists in the field of second language learning had been referring to **language interference,** the tendency for a person's first language to influence the errors produced in a second language. Since John Oller and Seid Ziahosseiny reported that such interference was greatest when the differences between the two languages were minimal (186), it was only logical to assume that speaking AAE might interfere greatly with learning SWE. Therefore, when compositionists referred to dialect interference in writing, they were applying, by analogy, what they thought held true for other language arts (Hartwell 101–6).

Add to this commonsense approach a plethora of studies purportedly showing that AAE "causes" SWE errors in students' writing, and writing teachers who cite dialect interference seem to have an airtight case. Indeed, in the 1970s one researcher estimated that dialect interference accounted for 40 percent of the errors in AAE speakers' writing (Fasold).

But the dialect interference hypothesis has not fulfilled its promise. First of all, it assumes that we write the way we speak. If this assumption were true, Patrick Hartwell observes, "then written English could not be a functioning national language in Nigeria, Australia, India, the Philippines, Liberia, Kenya, and Ireland, much less Texas and Maine" (103). Consider the word *sign*. Regardless of dialect, virtually no one pronounces *sign* like the first four sounds in *significant*. Yet nearly all of us learn to write *sign* because that spelling preserves the meaning rather than the sound. "It seems likely, then," Wolfram, Adger, and Christian observe, "that a child who pronounces *toof* [in AAE] can adjust to the standard spelling *tooth* as well as another child who says *tuff* [in Standard English] learns to spell it *tough*" (136).

The fact that we see relatively few instances of AAE-related spelling (see Chapter 2) certainly calls into question the dialect interference hypothesis.

The hypothesis also lacks sufficient empirical support. As Hartwell notes in his review, most of the studies of dialect interference are poorly designed:

> [W]riting samples are gathered from black students and analyzed for errors "caused by" dialect interference, usually without verifying the features of the students' spoken dialect, without considering control samples from speakers of other dialects, and without considering other relevant variables (such as reading ability, for example). (107)

Even when a study is adequately designed, it rarely produces the expected results. The work of Marcia Farr Whiteman is a case in point. Whiteman and her colleagues examined thousands of papers written by black and white students; they also interviewed black AAE speakers and white speakers of nonstandard Southern White American English. Although they found that black writers omitted -s and -ed endings in writing more often than white writers did, many AAE features (e.g., *ain't*, double negatives, habitual *be*) hardly ever showed up in the writing. Most surprising, there was no predictable relationship between how often students omitted -s or -ed endings in speech and how often they did so in writing. In fact, Whiteman discovered that many white students omitted the verbal -s twice as often in their writing as they did in their speech. In addition, they omitted the plural -s in their writing even though they almost never did when speaking (158–59). Thus, Whiteman concluded that dialect was "not solely responsible for the occurrence of nonstandard features in writing" (164). In other words, the dialect interference hypothesis could not explain why some AAE features did not turn up in writing or why others turned up in the writing of students who did not use them in their speech.

Since the publication of Whiteman's findings, the dialect interference hypothesis has lost much of its luster for composition researchers.[1] Earlier, reading and second language researchers also had become disenchanted with the notion of interference, in part because it explained so little.[2] For instance, why doesn't dialect tend to interfere with reading comprehension? And why does "language interference" account for no more than half of the errors in second language learning studies? (Ellis; Hartwell 105–6). Moreover, how significant could it be when listening, reading, speaking, and writing well encompass so much more than knowing standard grammar, pronunciation, and spelling? Despite these questions, the dialect interference hypothesis is alive and well in many English classrooms across the United States, as illustrated by this line from the mission statement of the writing program at a Chicago university: "The writing programs . . . bring students with second language and *dialect interference problems* [our emphasis] into the mainstream of standard written English. . . ."

How Does AAE Influence Writing?

So if dialect does not interfere with thinking or writing, how do we explain the preponderance of SWE errors in so many AAE speakers' papers? Certainly, the writing samples in Appendix A attest to the *influence* of AAE on everything from words to rhetorical patterns. But, if AAE does not interfere, *how* does it influence writing? The following hypotheses attempt to answer this question.

The Print Code Hypothesis

When he attacks the dialect interference hypothesis in his 1980 article, Hartwell proposes a counterexplanation for the AAE features in students' papers. Citing studies of strong and weak readers, he argues that students who speak AAE experience the same problem other developing writers do: unfamiliarity with certain conventions of written texts. It is primarily through reading, Hartwell contends, that students learn about these conventions—from spelling and punctuation to tone and inference. When they are not certain about an aspect of this "print code," they fall back on their oral resources (108–9).

In the case of AAE speakers, those oral resources happen to be nonstandard, and that makes all the difference. When white middle-class students fall back on *their* oral resources, a teacher may barely notice the oral features in their writing because their speech is so similar to SWE. In contrast, when AAE speakers follow suit, the oral features in their writing stand out as "errors" because their speech is so distinct from SWE. Imagine, for example, two students who do not know how to refer to a cousin's house while attempting to write SWE. The white middle-class student writes, "My cousins' house," misplacing the apostrophe. At the same time, the AAE speaker writes, "My cousin house," because *cousin* does not require a possessive ending in AAE. Both instances are SWE errors, but the white student's error seems less egregious because it still sounds like SWE. Thus, neither group's spoken dialect interferes with writing SWE, but the AAE group's way of speaking yields many words, sentences, and even rhetorical patterns that are inconsistent with SWE.

Interdialectal Hypothesis

Although the print code hypothesis distinguishes dialect influence from dialect interference, it does not adequately explain the surprising trend Whiteman found in her data—the tendency for white and black writers to drop endings in their writing even when they retain them in their speech. As Whiteman notes, however, research on first and second language learning suggests that speakers, regardless of dialect, tend to drop endings to simplify the task of learning a new language. And it just so happens that people learning a new language drop the same endings that people do when learning how to write (163). Therefore, Whiteman concludes, "It is quite plausible that relatively inexperienced writers use a similar 'redundancy reduction' strategy in their attempt to learn a new code (writing)" (163). If so, some SWE errors that look like AAE features are not. They are merely evidence of trying to learn a dialect that no one speaks—Standard Written English.

Such a hypothesis could easily explain hypercorrections such as the plural *mens* cited in Chapter 2 or the construction *its would be* in a student's composition cited by Wolfram, Adger, and Christian. Having identified the student as a speaker of AAE, they speculate that teachers had admonished the student for omitting *is* in sentences like *She here*. As a result, they conclude, "the unnecessary addition of *s* on *its* in the case of *its would be* may represent an unconscious effort to avoid the mistake of leaving *is* or *are* out, but without a full understanding of the structure in question" (132).

From this perspective, AAE speakers, like people learning a new language, construct their own **interdialect** by simplifying SWE forms and overgeneralizing SWE rules. Thus, unlike the dialect interference or print code hypotheses, the interdialectal hypothesis can explain how AAE speakers occasionally produce forms that do not exist in Standard or African American English. As Charles Coleman (498), Eleanor Kutz (393), and others point out, the interdialectal hypothesis permits teachers to see some SWE errors as learning in progress, as signs of growth.

What Other Factors Account for AAE Features in Writing?

The print code and interdialectal hypotheses predict that when students do not know an SWE form, they will substitute an (AAE) oral form such as *two boy* or construct an interdialectal form such as *two mens*. But these hypotheses ignore two other possibilities: (1) that the students know the SWE form or (2) if they don't, they don't want to use it. These possibilities are real, as suggested by the composing process and language attitude hypotheses.

The Composing Process Hypothesis

While research indicates that AAE does not interfere with writing, the very act of writing can. In his seminal essay "The Study of Error," David Bartholomae explains:

> Errors in writing may be caused by interference from the act of writing itself, from the difficulty of moving a pen across the page quickly enough to keep up with words in the writer's mind, or

> from the difficulty of recalling and producing conventions that are necessary for producing print rather than speech, conventions of spelling, orthography, punctuation, capitalization and so on. (259)

Add to these constraints some of the higher-level demands that Linda Flower and John Hayes identified in their groundbreaking research on the composing process: thinking about the audience, retrieving information, synthesizing it, and so on. To borrow their metaphor, the composing process is a juggling act, and too often inexperienced writers drop a ball (41).

Therefore, even when AAE speakers know an SWE rule, they may violate it because of the conceptual and physical demands of composing. In other words, their performance betrays their competence. Their communicative **competence** is everything they know about language—all the rules for grammar, pronunciation, and meaning; all the vocabulary; their reading and writing skills; their ability to expand their own language and learn other languages. On the other hand, their **performance** is what and how they are able to communicate, at any given time, in the form required—spoken, written, signed, or sung.

Bartholomae contends that most SWE errors are "rooted in the difficulty of performance" rather than lack of competence (264). To illustrate his point, he cites a student's essay that is riddled with SWE errors. Here is an excerpt:

> Let me tell you about the situation first of all what happen was that I got suspense from school. For thing that I fell was out of my control sometime, but it taught me alot about respondability of a growing man. The school suspense me for being late ten time. (260)

At first glance, some of these SWE errors look like AAE forms, especially *happen, thing, ten time*. But when Bartholomae asked the author, John, to read aloud, noting any errors, John read the passage as follows:

> Let me tell you about the situation [John comes to a full stop.] first of all what happen*ed* was that I got *suspended* from school [no full stop] for things that I *felt* was out of my control some-

time, but it taught me a lot about *responsibility* of a growing man. The school *suspended* me for being late ten time*s*. (261–62)

Surprisingly, John corrected almost every SWE error as he read aloud. He did not, however, realize that there *were* errors on the paper or that he had corrected them. What his reading suggests is that he is not paying enough attention to sound–letter correspondences when he reads or writes. In other words, most of his so-called errors are **miscues.** He doesn't need grammar drills; he needs proofreading skills (Bartholomae 262). As Barbara Walvoord observes, ineffective proofreading is a common "performance-based" problem (236), and teachers should distinguish it from the "knowledge-based" problems that the print code and interdialectal hypotheses address.

The Language Attitude Hypothesis

The composing process hypothesis reminds us that we should not consider SWE errors out of context; we should examine them within the context of the entire composing process, from prewriting to proofreading. But we should also view them within their cultural context. In *Students' Right to Their Own Language*, the Conference on College Composition and Communication (CCCC) explains:

> Since dialect is not separate from culture, but an intrinsic part of it, accepting a new dialect means accepting a new culture; rejecting one's native dialect is to some extent a rejection of one's culture. Therefore the question of whether or not students will change their dialect involves their acceptance of a new—and possibly strange or hostile—set of cultural values. (6)

This notion of cultural conflict has also been articulated by scholars such as James Paul Gee, Ngugi wa Thiong'o, and Frantz Fanon.

From this cultural perspective, we can understand why some AAE speakers continue to write AAE in their school compositions. They recognize that white middle- and upper-class Americans constitute the ruling elite in the United States and that this ruling elite privileges Standard English (both spoken and written) while stigmatizing AAE. Since these AAE speakers associate SWE with the culture of a "strange or hostile" group, they resist efforts to teach them SWE. In fact, as Signithia Fordham and John Obgu have documented, such students may resist schooling in general because they believe African Americans who excel in school are "acting white" or just bumping their heads against a racist society's glass ceiling.

We can see the same cultural dynamic in research on second language learning. In the 1970s, Robert Gardner, Wallace Lambert, John Oller, and others documented the importance of students' attitudes toward the target language (L2) as well as their own (L1). Gardner and Lambert for example, discovered that people who had positive feelings about the members of the L2 culture were highly motivated to learn a second language. Likewise, Oller, Hudson, and Liu found that positive attitudes toward oneself, the L1 group, and the L2 group facilitated learning a second language. Research also indicates, however, that cultural assimilation is not necessary to master a second language. Sometimes the desire to attain a career (Lukmani) or simply to make oneself understood (Macnamara) will suffice. Together, these findings support Stephen Krashen's affective filter hypothesis, which predicts that people acquire a second language most easily when they are motivated, possess a positive self-image, and have a low level of anxiety (9–32).

While researchers (e.g., J. Coleman; Teweles) are still trying to clarify the relative importance of different types of motivation, there is enough evidence to justify applying the preceding concepts to speakers of AAE. We would expect more resistance in compulsory primary and secondary schools than in colleges since most college students are pursuing careers that require Standard English. Even at the college level, however, we may find significant differences in motivation. In a recent study, first-year college students who spoke both Standard and African American English considered Standard English important for success in school and on the job. But, as Smitherman would say, some saw Standard English as a language of "wider, not whiter" communication (*Talkin That Talk* 161), a lingua franca that ensures that "everyone, regardless of racial background, can communicate with one another" (Redd, "How I Got" 9–10). Meanwhile, some of the others characterized Standard English as "white."

At the college level, we may also find evidence of **stereotype threat.** According to psychologist Claude Steele, stereotype threat is "the threat of being viewed through the lens of a negative stereotype, or the fear of doing something that would inadvertently confirm that stereotype." This sense of social mistrust may cause some African American writers, whether they speak only AAE or not, to perform poorly on writing tests (especially standardized ones) because they fear that their scores will confirm negative stereotypes about African American students' writing.

Such attitudes are not the only cultural barriers to mastery of SWE. Teachers' attitudes toward AAE are a common obstacle with far-reaching consequences. Research suggests that a teacher's attitude toward a student's speech is "the most powerful single factor" in determining a teacher's expectations for that student (Labov, "Can Reading" 49). Research also indicates that a teacher's expectations can stimulate or stifle a student's performance (Tauber). Thus, a teacher's negative attitude toward AAE may lead to negative expectations, and those negative expectations may hinder students' mastery of SWE. For instance, if a teacher believes that AAE is a sign of genetic inferiority or verbal deprivation, the students may assume that they are not smart enough to master SWE. Or if a teacher believes that AAE interferes with mastering SWE, the students may hesitate to say or write anything of substance for fear that AAE will take control— hence the verdict in the 1979 "Black English Case" (*Martin Luther King Junior Elementary School Children v. Ann Arbor School District Board*). In this landmark case, the court ruled that the teachers' "negative attitudes toward the children's language [AAE] led to negative expectations of the children which turned into self-fulfilling prophecies" (Smitherman, "What Go" 44). This verdict applies to even the most skilled teachers. Citing Sondra Perl and Nancy Wilson's findings, Marcia Farr and Harvey Daniels observe that "even the best available teaching methods can fail when implemented by teachers who lack genuine, fundamental appreciation for what students can already do with language" (52).

On the other hand, teachers' positive attitudes toward AAE may facilitate the acquisition of SWE, as Angle found. Research on effective African American teachers attributes much of the teachers' success to their positive attitudes toward their students' culture and their efforts to link the culture of the school to the culture of the students' homes or community (Ball, "Community-Based"; Ball and Lardner; Foster; Ladson-Billings; Moore). Indeed, after observing successful teachers in community literacy programs, Arnetha Ball listed the following principles first in her list of twelve successful teaching strategies ("Playin' the Dozens"):

1. Readjust attitudes.

2. Confront racial insecurities and prejudices.

3. Hold high expectations and communicate them.

Teachers motivated by these principles see AAE speakers' communication skills as a resource for teaching academic literacy, not as an impediment.

Summary

In her classic book *Errors and Expectations*, Mina Shaughnessy describes the plight of the basic writer. She laments, "such was the quality of their instruction that no one saw the intelligence of their mistakes or thought to harness that intelligence in the service of learning" (11). The same can be said of many AAE speakers. For years the SWE errors in their papers were attributed to a lack of intelligence or dialect interference. Eventually, researchers began to see instead the resourcefulness of writers drawing on their oral repertoire when the SWE form escaped them—or the progress of writers inventing new forms to approximate SWE. More recently, researchers have investigated SWE errors in a wider context. They have found that the composing process and language attitudes can affect students' ability to write SWE. These findings suggest that writing teachers should take Shaughnessy's advice: instead of trying to trace all of a student's SWE errors to a particular source, they should search for "evidence of a number of interacting influences" (10). At the same time, they should remember that even SWE errors that look the same may have "different histories" (Morrow 165).

Notes

1. A recent analysis of African American students' "think aloud" writing protocols has revealed even more complex dynamics than Whiteman's study did. AAE features occurred in four patterns: (a) spoken only, (b) spoken into writing, (c) spoken but corrected in writing, and (d) written but not spoken (Mix 323, 327).
2. John Rickford, however, claims that, in the field of second language learning, dialect interference is "making a comeback," reconceptualized under a new name: *language transfer*. The concept has proved useful in developing students' awareness of language differences ("Language" 15).

Suggested Readings

Bartholomae, David. "The Study of Error." *College Composition and Communication* 31 (1980): 253–69.

Baugh, John. *Out of the Mouths of Slaves: African American Language and Educational Malpractice.* Austin: U of Texas P, 1999.

Conference on College Composition and Communication (CCCC). *Students' Right to Their Own Language.* Spec. issue of *College Composition and Communication,* 25 (1974).

Dandy, Evelyn Baker. *Black Communications: Breaking Down the Barriers.* Chicago: African American Images, 1991.

Delpit, Lisa, and Joanne Kilgour Dowdy, eds. *The Skin That We Speak: Thoughts on Language and Culture in the Classroom.* New York: New Press, 2002.

Farr, Marcia, and Harvey Daniels. *Language Diversity and Writing Instruction.* Urbana, IL: ERIC Clearinghouse on Reading and Communication Skills, 1986. ERIC Doc. ED274996.

Green, Lisa J. *African American English: A Linguistic Introduction.* Cambridge: Cambridge UP, 2002.

Labov, William. "Academic Ignorance and Black Intelligence." *Atlantic Monthly* June 1972. 3 June 2003 <www.theatlantic.com>.

Richardson, Elaine. *African American Literacies*. London: Routledge, 2003.

Shaughnessy, Mina. *Errors and Expectations: A Guide for the Teacher of Basic Writing*. New York: Oxford UP, 1977.

Smitherman, Geneva. *Talkin and Testifyin: The Language of Black America*. 1977. Detroit: Wayne State UP, 1986.

CHAPTER FOUR

How Can AAE Speakers Become Effective SWE Writers?

Consciously or unconsciously, the hypotheses in Chapter 3 shape how teachers of AAE speakers approach the teaching of SWE. As a result, some teachers choose not to teach SWE at all. For instance, persuaded by the deficit hypotheses, some don't bother to teach SWE because they think AAE speakers are too dumb or deprived to master it. Meanwhile, others—motivated by the language attitude hypothesis—refrain from teaching SWE rather than force AAE speakers to adopt "a strange or hostile set of cultural values." At the same time—citing the composing process hypothesis—some argue that focusing on SWE skills will stifle students' fluency and creativity, so they just encourage students to "edit out" SWE errors on their own. Finally, confused by conflicting theories, other teachers simply give up.

As you can imagine, with these laissez-faire approaches, virtually the only AAE speakers who learn to "edit out" SWE errors are those who intensively read and write SWE texts outside of school (as the print code hypothesis would predict). Students have to *recognize* SWE errors in order to "edit them out," and such recognition normally requires some sort of instruction when Standard English is not the language of the home (Noguchi 14).

Fortunately, the hypotheses in Chapter 3 have also inspired a variety of strategies for teaching AAE speakers Standard Written English. The strategies range from the traditional approach, which excludes AAE from the curriculum and classroom, to the bridge approach, which uses AAE to build a "bridge" to SWE. Keep in mind, however, that teaching SWE forms is only one aspect of writing instruction. The general principles derived from composition research also apply to teaching writing to speakers of AAE. Like other composition students, AAE speakers need to read carefully, write frequently, address different audiences for meaningful purposes, study models of writing in progress and in print, collaborate with peers, confer with the teacher, and, of course, devote time to prewriting, drafting, and revising.

Although we recognize that some teachers combine strategies, for the sake of clarity we present in this chapter five contrasting approaches to teaching AAE speakers SWE. First, we describe the teaching philosophy, instructional activities, and assessment methods of a particular approach. Then we examine the supporting and opposing evidence.

To illustrate each approach, we refer to sample assignments (see Appendix B) as well as scenarios showing how teachers representing each of the five approaches respond to the same AAE feature. Although the assignments and scenarios address the needs of a first-year college student, a few incorporate teaching methods tested at a lower level because the teachers are striving to meet the student at the student's level of SWE acquisition, regardless of grade level.

All of the assignments and scenarios focus on the lack of a present-tense -s ending on third-person singular verbs. We have chosen this feature (1) because it frequently shows up in AAE speakers' writing, (2) because in academic writing the omission of the verbal -s is more stigmatizing than many other AAE features, and (3) because many of us find teaching AAE speakers SWE grammar more difficult than teaching them SWE rhetoric.

In the five scenarios, the teachers respond to the inconsistent use of verbal -s in the following passage by an eighteen-year-old whom we will call Jamal:

> Jealousy is a cause of prejudice against style of dress. For example, a girl hate another girl because the other girl can afford designer clothes. The girl get jealous because she can't afford designer clothes, so she becomes prejudice against the girl and not interact with her.

Now, beginning with the traditional approach, let's see how five different teachers might respond.

The Traditional Approach

In her history of the *Harbrace College Handbook*, Debra Hawhee defines traditional composition pedagogy (also known as **current traditional rhetoric**) as "a product oriented approach that seeks to secure a mastery of finite grammatical rules and 'correct' usage" (505). This approach dates back to the second half of the nineteenth century, when the focus of American writing instruction shifted from rhetoric to correctness (Connors 65). But the approach became entrenched in most composition textbooks in 1941 with the publication of the *Harbrace College Handbook*. Now in its fifteenth edition, *Harbrace* is still the "cornerstone" of the traditional approach (Hawhee 505). Other well-known examples of the traditional approach are the "compensatory education programs" that the U.S. government funded in the 1960s to teach "culturally deprived" African Americans how to read and write. Many of their pedagogical strategies are now marketed in textbook/workbook series such as SRA's DISTAR Language, a program that teaches basic literacy skills through teacher-directed drills (Science Research Associates).

Philosophy

Although the traditional approach has become more process oriented since the 1980s, the underlying philosophy has barely changed over the years. Central to its philosophy is the concept of **immersion,** the assumption that students must be immersed in Standard English to avoid dialect interference or to compensate for the lack of standard speech in the home. Thus, in the traditional classroom, Standard English reigns supreme. It is considered not only "good" or "proper" English but also a ticket to success. As Richardson observes, the traditional approach espouses a "rhetoric of meritocracy," whose "central tenet is that anyone can pull him/herself 'up' by the bootstraps and get 'a good job' through education and hard work. In other words, if students clean up their language and learn how to read and write, they can be successful" (*African American* 20).

Instruction

To see how a traditional teacher might respond to Jamal, let us visit the classroom of Mary Hall. Seeking to immerse her students in Standard English, Hall attends not only to their writing but also to their speech. Therefore, even though she understands what Jamal is saying, she interrupts to correct him if he says, for instance, "the boy know" while speaking in class or reading aloud.

To strengthen Jamal's control of SWE subject-verb agreement, Hall also provides explicit instruction and practice, practice, practice. Whether during a class, conference, video, or online slide show, she presents the rules for SWE agreement, just as the *Harbrace* does (Whitten, Horner, and Webb 62):

Make a verb agree in number with its subject.
As you study the following rules and examples, remember that *-s* (or *-es*) marks plural nouns but singular verbs (those present-tense verbs with third-person singular subjects):

subject + *s*	OR	verb + *s*
The egotists like attention.		The egotist likes attention.
Tomatoes ripen best in the sun.		A tomato ripens best in the sun.

Note: Be sure that you do not omit the *-s* on the third-person singular form of the verb: The telephone **rings** constantly. (NOT *ring*)

To reinforce these rules, exercises will follow (see the sample exercise in Appendix B). Consistent with the traditional emphasis on speaking and writing, for example, *Harbrace* includes a subject-verb agreement exercise that directs students to read aloud "correct" sentences, emphasizing the italicized words. "If any sentence sounds wrong," the authors advise, "read it aloud two or three more times so that you will gain practice in saying and hearing the correct forms" (Whitten, Horner, and Webb 67). The next exercise asks students to select "the correct form" of the verb from a pair, following "the rules of formal English" (67).

Jamal completes such exercises orally or with a peer group during class, or he does so individually on paper or online for homework. If Hall sees that Jamal continues to omit the *-s* in his essays, she may also ask him to rewrite a model sentence such as

Helen likes to solve physics problems using different third-person subjects: *My father likes to solve physics problems; John likes to solve physics problems,* and so on (see Smitherman, *Talkin and Testifyin* 209).

Since Hall recognizes that reading influences writing, she assigns many texts, all narrated in the standard. Thus, she scrupulously avoids works such as Zora Neale Hurston's *Their Eyes Were Watching God* that have "too much" AAE. With the exception of an essay or two written by an African American, Hall's texts consist mainly of "classic" works by white writers. Hall asks students to write about these texts, following the steps of the composing process: plan, draft, and revise. The students' writing at all stages of the composing process, however, must conform to the rules of Standard Written English.

Assessment

Hall relies on standardized testing (multiple-choice items and timed essays) for placement and exit examinations. When she reviews the test results, she pays special attention to the subscores for mechanics. She gives mechanics the same level of attention when she evaluates Jamal's course work, for she marks and deducts points in every draft for every SWE error, whether it is AAE related or not. In fact, because of the stigma attached to AAE grammar, she penalizes Jamal more heavily for his AAE-related errors.

Research

So is there evidence to support Hall's pedagogical approach? Consider first Hall's preoccupation with SWE errors.

STIGMA AND SUCCESS

Numerous usage surveys show that AAE is stigmatized in the workplace (e.g., Beason; Leonard and Gilsdorf; Hairston). Professionals report that they find most bothersome sentences such as *Jones don't think it is acceptable, There has never been no one here like that woman, Calhoun has went after every prize in the university,* and *When we was in the planning stages of the project, we underestimated costs* (Hairston 800–806). But while these surveys document that AAE can lock doors to many careers, this finding does not apply to all careers (Botan and Smitherman). Above all, the research does not prove that SWE will automatically open doors for African Americans, doors that are often shut tight by racism.

IMMERSION

On the other hand, research on first and second language learning shows that immersion in a new language is the most effective way to master it. Like Hall, McWhorter insists that Standard English should be the official language of the curriculum and the classroom since every hour spent engaging AAE in the classroom is "one less hour spent immersed in the standard English dialect" (*Word* 245). On linguistic and practical grounds, however, Rickford questions whether immersion techniques apply to AAE:

> For one thing, immersion seems to be more successful in the acquisition of a second language rather than a second dialect, where extensive overlaps in vocabulary, phonology, and grammar can cause speakers to miss subtle but significant differences between their own and the target variety. Secondly, where would SE immersion occur? The effect of exposure to SE via noninteractive media like radio and TV is apparently minimal. It is rather implausible to propose that SE be used exclusively in schools, including among AAVE-speaking friends. Immersion in SE in classrooms is already the method of choice in the overwhelming majority of U.S. schools. If it's so promising, why hasn't it produced better results? ("Language" 12)

Van Keulen, Weddington, and DeBose also point out the impracticality of immersion for AAE speakers. Because so many AAE speakers are placed in remedial and special education classes, they have little opportunity to interact with Standard English–speaking classmates. Moreover, when AAE speakers return home, residential segregation ensures that most will rarely hear Standard English in their neighborhood (191).

Even McWhorter concedes that by their late teens many AAE speakers have passed the stage where they can "pick up" a new language or dialect simply through immersion. Moreover, he believes that children should be allowed to speak AAE in class while they are absorbing the standard because research shows that correcting their speech is useless or harmful (*Word* 248–49, 253). Indeed, one researcher found that when teachers relentlessly corrected African American children's classroom speech, the children scored *lower* on reading tests (Piestrup). While observing classes, Smitherman (*Talkin and Testifyin* 217–18), Dandy (1–2), and Delpit ("What" 17–18, 24) also found that constant correction could have devastating psychological as well as educational consequences. After watching one teacher correct a boy's oral reading, Dandy remarked:

> Her constant interruptions broke the story line, emphasized reading as a sounding out process, brought attention to reading word by word, and much more seriously, demoralized Joey in front of his peers. Joey was correct in reading for meaning, so he should *not* have been interrupted. (2–3)

Thus, we cannot expect correcting students' speech to improve their speaking or reading or writing.

EXPLICIT TEACHING OF GRAMMAR

But what about Hall's grammar lessons? Will explicit instruction in grammar help Jamal write Standard English? Because writing is a more conscious use of language than speaking, we might expect Jamal to profit from grammatical analysis, at least while revising or proofreading. Yet the majority of studies suggest that teaching grammar of any kind does not improve the quality of students' academic writing and has had "at best, mixed results even for teaching correctness" (Hillocks 140, 248–49).

The verdict, however, is not final. Rei Noguchi points out that most of those studies never confirmed that the students actually learned what was taught or attempted to apply it while revising or proofreading (7–8). In his review of the research, Richard Hudson also notes that most studies that have produced positive results are "clearly focused on one particular area of grammar . . . which correlates with an aspect of writing where children need help" (4). These observations suggest that explicit teaching of grammar may improve AAE speakers' command of SWE if teachers improve the focus and methods of the lessons.

Perhaps a clear focus and method explain why Jane Torrey reported positive effects from "a worksheet-based, explicit instructional program" and why Ball did as well when she replicated Torrey's experiment (Ball, "Language" 23). Torrey and Ball focused their instruction on the -s ending in Standard English. For instance, they showed second-grade AAE speakers pictures with the sentences *Two boys run_* or *One boy_ runs,* where the third-person singular -s ending was highlighted in red or a blank signaled its absence. Then, after explaining the SWE rules, they showed the children pairs of sentences with or without the red -s ending. On their worksheets, the children wrote an -s in the blank if they thought one was needed and read aloud their sentences (32). While Torrey reported significant gains in children's use of the *is* contraction (as in *She's jumping*), Ball reported significant gains in their use of the singular verb -s ending as well. Therefore, Ball recommends that teachers provide "clear instructions, definitions, and rules when making explanations to students about the use of grammatical forms they do not generally use at a level of metalinguistic awareness" (42–43).

Unfortunately, we do not know whether the children in Torrey's and Ball's studies transferred their learning to composing. What we do know is that African American students tend to prefer such explicit grammar teaching. Delpit reports that many African American students and parents value the English teacher who spells out the rules of Standard English because otherwise they cannot gain access to that code of power. She explains, "If you are not already a participant in the culture of power, being told explicitly the rules of that culture makes acquiring power easier" ("Silenced" 25). Though she dislikes its narrow focus on basic skills, Delpit attributes much of DISTAR's success in the inner city to its "explicitness and direct instruction": unlike some "progressive" critical thinking programs, it breaks down reading and writing skills for children instead of assuming that they had already learned the fundamentals in a white middle-class home ("Silenced" 30). Delpit also cites a study by Siddle, who found that, of all her teaching strategies, "the intervention that produced the most positive changes in her African American students' writing was a 'mini-lesson' consisting of direct instruction about some standard writing convention" ("Silenced" 33). Therefore, we should not assume that AAE speakers won't profit from the direct teaching of grammar simply because studies suggest that white students don't.

GRAMMAR EXERCISES

Delpit does not, however, advocate that AAE speakers fill out "page after page of 'skills sheets,'" divorced from any meaningful communicative activity ("Silenced" 44). After all, a curriculum devoted to grammar and spelling exercises takes time away from actual composing—writing paragraphs, essays, and stories—and misleads students into assuming that "good writing" is "good grammar." It runs the risk of boring students while stifling critical thinking and self-expression. Moreover, the only type of grammar exercise that has been proven to improve the quality of writing is the sentence-combining exercise, yet even it does not consistently reduce the SWE error rate (Hillocks 142–44).

Another common problem with traditional grammar exercises is delayed feedback. When students write exercises for homework, they may not discover for days or weeks whether they have chosen the right answers. (Indeed, they may have practiced writing the wrong answer!) To avoid this problem, some teachers assign in-class, computer-assisted, or online exercises so that students can receive immediate feedback. It is worth noting that students in successful studies such as Torrey's and Ball's received immediate feedback from the researchers during the lessons.

MARKING EVERY ERROR

When Hall gives students feedback on their essays, she red-marks every SWE error, especially those assumed to be related to AAE. Yet research suggests that such error hunting is overkill: there is no evidence that marking every error is more effective than focusing on a few patterns of error. Worse, error hunting can produce negative effects by overwhelming students, leaving them wondering where to begin or feeling discouraged about writing (Hillocks 164, 166–68). Finally, teachers who mark every SWE error often overlook the quality of an essay's content, organization, or style (Smitherman, *Talkin and Testifyin* 229–30).

This imbalance is also a weakness of the standardized tests that Hall uses: some of the tests do not even require writing, and those that do generally give disproportionate weight to SWE correctness (Wolfram, Adger, and Christian 138). Farr and Daniels argue that this concern for correctness is illogical and unfair when viewed in the context of other academic subjects:

> A piece of student writing is judged "bad" when perhaps every tenth word contains an error or deviates somehow from standard written language. But notice what a lofty standard of correctness is being applied here. In any other school subject . . . 90 percent accuracy is considered *excellent*. . . . The fact is that we hold to a higher standard of perfection in the mechanics of writing than in any other school subject. And this anomaly punishes— drastically and disproportionately—students whose home dialect happens to differ even slightly from the dialect approved by the school. (82)

To sum up, the explicit instruction of the traditional approach may help AAE speakers learn SWE when the lessons are focused and provide immediate feedback. It is not clear, however, that students will transfer their newfound knowledge to composing. Furthermore, the teacher's preoccupation with SWE errors can lead to too much correcting and drilling.

The Second Dialect Approach

Some writing teachers have modified the traditional approach by adapting methods from the teaching of English as a Second Language (ESL) to the teaching of SWE to AAE speakers. Known as the English as a Second Dialect (ESD) approach, this approach was pioneered by Irwin Feigenbaum, Carol Reed, and others in the early 1970s. Reed's experiment at Brooklyn College became a model for others interested in ESD methodology (Gilyard, "African" 638). Reed and her colleagues describe the ESD approach as follows:

> The way in which our approach differs from traditional peda-
> gogical methodology is that it utilizes the speech patterns of the
> students in an attempt to help them gain facility in Standard En-
> glish. . . . [W]e are merely trying to improve the students' linguis-
> tic versatility, thereby enabling them to perform effectively in a
> variety of speech communities and social settings. (Language
> Curriculum Research Group 174)

Despite her explanation, critics assumed that Reed was teaching
AAE when in fact she was using AAE in the classroom and curriculum to highlight the differences between AAE and the standard (Gilyard, "African" 638–39). Twenty-five years later the
same misunderstanding ignited the furor over Oakland's Standard English Proficiency Program (SEP). Like nearly sixteen other
California school districts, Oakland's school district also employed
ESD methodology (O. Taylor 170).

Philosophy

The ESD approach appeals particularly to bidialectalists because
it reflects a **contrastive rhetoric** that views all languages as cultural phenomena, each with its unique linguistic and rhetorical
conventions. Drawing on the dialect interference hypothesis, the
ESD approach assumes that the conventions of a student's first
language will influence how that student writes a second language (Connor 199). The ESD approach, however, presumes that
AAE speakers can avoid interference if the teacher heightens students' **metalinguistic awareness** of AAE-SWE differences by high-
lighting those differences—just as ESL teachers highlight
differences between languages. In addition, the ESD approach
promotes the ability to **code-switch** from one dialect to another
as the situation demands. Hence, it presents AAE as a rule-governed variety of language that students should preserve as their
"home language" while acquiring SWE as their "school language."

   Borrowing once again from ESL pedagogy, the ESD approach
also assumes that language learning moves naturally from listening to speaking and then to reading and writing—i.e., from recognition to reproduction (H. Taylor 107, 121). Therefore, it embraces oral activities as well as reading and writing to strengthen
AAE speakers' control of SWE.

Instruction

Because the ESD approach highlights differences between AAE and SWE, the cornerstone of ESD instruction is **contrastive analysis,** the juxtaposition of features of two languages. Before contrasting AAE and SWE, however, David Su, an ESD teacher, contrasts AAE with other dialects and languages. He compares, for example, Russian *Ona umnaya* ("She smart") with AAE "She smart" to demonstrate that omitting the linking verb *be* in AAE is perfectly logical. Or he compares AAE and Appalachian English to show that many whites also speak a nonstandard dialect (Reed 291).

Once Jamal and his classmates understand the relativity of standards of correctness, Su starts to contrast AAE and SWE. Through careful examination of his students' diagnostic essays, he has already identified the AAE features that seem to interfere with the students' efforts to produce SWE. Now he helps the students discover these features inductively by having them discuss the same passage, written first in AAE and then in SWE, while listing and grouping the features on the board (Reed 297–302). Then he encourages the students to use their intuition to analyze and predict the SWE problems they might encounter while writing academic essays (Reed 291, 293). Clearly, Su never forgets that, unlike second language learners, AAE speakers already know a great deal about Standard Written English.

Since Jamal frequently omits the third-person -*s*, Su frequently assigns Jamal additional work in contrastive analysis. For instance, Su asks Jamal to complete a discrimination drill that begins as follows (H. Taylor 112; see Appendix B for another sample exercise):

Read the following sentence pairs and identify the differing words:

Penny like to ride around town.

Penny likes to ride around town.

In addition to analyzing such contrasts, Jamal and his classmates practice code-switching in speech and writing through **audiolingual pattern practice.** One example is the following cloze drill (H. Taylor 114–15):

Supply the deleted letters or words in the following sentences:

He won't come straight out and tell you what he want_.

She enjoy_ college life but she wouldn't mind another year of high school.

Jamal can complete such drills in a lab after class using computer or audiolingual equipment. But instead of relying on monotonous and decontextualized drills, Su might ask Jamal to translate into SWE an excerpt of AAE dialogue from Lorraine Hansberry's *A Raisin in the Sun* (H. Taylor 118–19). Or he might "disguise" a pattern drill by asking Jamal to edit one feature at a time (e.g., subject-verb agreement) in his or other students' papers (Reed 292). In addition, Su might ask Jamal and his classmates to practice code-switching through role-playing or dialogues (Arthur 272).

If Jamal is playing a role that demands Standard English, Su will question Jamal's use of an inappropriate AAE feature. Su never corrects Jamal's speech, however, during oral reading or class discussion. Instead, he **models** the SWE usage. Therefore, if Jamal says, "That boy know he wrong," Su will respond, "Yes, that boy know*s* he*'s* wrong" (Van Keulen, Weddington, and DeBose 189–90).

Assessment

Although Su administers his department's standardized placement and exit exams, he prefers his own writing assignments and assessments. When he asks Jamal to write poetry or fictional dialogues, Su treats the AAE in Jamal's writing as an appropriate vehicle for self-expression or realistic portrayal. When he evaluates Jamal's essays, however, Su undertakes an **error analysis.** First he distinguishes AAE features from other SWE errors. Then he acknowledges the learning-in-progress that hypercorrections and other interdialectal forms reveal (C. Coleman 498). Eventually, he deducts points for AAE-related features and other SWE errors, but only in Jamal's final drafts (Wilson 52). Unlike traditional teacher Mary Hall, Su applies the process model of prewriting, writing, and rewriting to assessment as well as instruction.

Research

CODE-SWITCHING

Su's primary objective is to help students master code-switching from AAE to SWE. As usage surveys (cited above) show, there are compelling reasons to switch from AAE to Standard English in the workplace. Critics of the ESD approach, however, point out that the code-switching in most ESD programs is one way, and thus the "rhetoric of difference" is still a rhetoric of deficiency. Engaging in a different sort of code-switching, Smitherman vividly explains why

> blacks quickly perceive that Black Dialect must not be all that systematic or beautiful, for after all, they is gon to have to give it up when they bees moving on up in "higher" social and economic groups. And, to add insult to injury, we all know that there ain no cultural enrichment or "language programs for the disadvantaged" in white, middle-class schools. That is, it is only upon blacks that the virtues and greatness of bi-dialectalism are inflicted. (*Talkin and Testifyin* 208)

Rebecca Howard agrees. She points out that "even though white dialects like Appalachian English are stigmatized in American society, they are not the object of code-switching pedagogy. Rather, it is the dialects of people of color that are to be switched from" (275–76). Therefore, Howard questions the right of the composition teacher to mandate switching from AAE to SWE. She recommends instead that teachers allow students to choose and that schools institute a course to teach students of *all* races about AAE (278–81).

CONTRASTIVE ANALYSIS

While code-switching is Su's goal, contrastive analysis is the primary means Su adopts to achieve that end. A number of programs like Su's that rely on contrastive analysis and/or audiolingual methods have reported considerable success in teaching SWE to AAE speakers. Among these programs are Kelli Harris-Wright's Bidialectal Communication Program in the DeKalb County school district in Georgia and Henry Parker and Marilyn Crist's Corporate English Program. Unfortunately, Parker and Crist do not offer hard evidence of their success (i.e., a comparison with a control group), and Harris-Wright reports an increase in reading (rather than writing) scores on the Iowa Test of Basic Skills (Rickford, "Ebonics" 276).

Hanni Taylor's study, however, provides empirical evidence of improvement in writing. In 1983, Taylor tested her Project Bidialectalism by using contrastive analysis and audiolingual drills with an experimental group of twenty African American college students while providing traditional instruction for a control group of twenty others. Taylor tracked the frequency of ten AAE features in the students' compositions. After eleven weeks, she witnessed a dramatic difference in third-person singular -*s* absence (as in *He walk*): The control group reduced their use of this AAE feature by 11 percent, but the experimental group reduced their use by 91.7 percent. The experimental group also reduced the number of hypercorrections by 66.7 percent, while the control group achieved a reduction of 38 percent. Although the frequency of other AAE features diminished only slightly, overall the experimental group reduced the number of AAE features by 59.3 percent. Meanwhile, the control group unexpectedly *increased* the number by 8.5 percent (149).

A more recent study evaluates another program that featured contrastive analysis, the Academic English Mastery Program in the Los Angeles Unified School District. During the 1998–99 school year, a random sample of 160 African American elementary students from the program achieved greater progress than a control group (a statistically significant gain of 2.50 versus 1.68 points) when they took a pretest and posttest of SWE proficiency. The research team observed that the ability to recognize linguistic differences between AAE and SWE (i.e., metalinguistic awareness) was associated with student progress (Maddahian and Sandamela).

Both Project Bidialectalism and the Academic English Mastery Program, however, combined contrastive analysis with other

methods such as culturally relevant teaching (see "The Culturally Appropriate Approach" section below). So it is impossible
to attribute all of their success to contrastive analysis or audiolingual methodology.

Wolfram and Schilling-Estes question the success of contrastive analysis on additional grounds. Although they maintain that
contrastive analysis "should underlie all programs for teaching
standard English," they find fault with the way most teachers
incorporate contrastive analysis. First, they observe that students
can quickly lose interest in the monotonous drills. Second, because the drills rely on explicit knowledge of rules, contrastive
analysis may serve students only when students can carefully
monitor their language, such as during formal writing. Third,
few contrastive lessons are truly bidialectal since (as noted above)
the role-playing and drills tend to move only from AAE to SWE,
not vice versa (289–95).

McWhorter objects to contrastive analysis for different reasons. He argues that it makes Standard English seem foreign to
AAE speakers. This impression, he claims, can hinder the learning of the standard because "a person is truly fluent in a language or dialect only when feeling it as a part of themselves, as
an expression of their soul" (*Word* 246). Therefore, he argues
that African American children will "pick up" the standard better without contrastive analysis, just as millions of bidialectal
African American adults have. He concedes, though, that African American adolescents and adults might profit from contrastive analysis since they are too old to easily learn the standard
from immersion and since contrastive analysis is appropriate for
a conscious process like writing (*Word* 247, 253).

ERROR ANALYSIS

Studies of error analysis (see Bartholomae; Shaughnessy) reveal
how much teachers like Su learn by tracing SWE errors to their
sources, AAE being only one possible source. Having reviewed
the research, Farr and Daniels conclude, "Analyzing error in this
way gives a teacher vital information that can guide instruction"
(80). Analyzing SWE errors can guide students as well. For instance, Karen Webb and Sloan Williams found that teaching AAE

speakers to analyze SWE errors in their essays in terms of AAE's topic-comment structure (see Chapter 2) helped students to understand *why* they had produced the errors. Consequently, the students could better edit their essays and monitor their language use.

To sum up, by providing error analysis, code-switching practice, and contrastive analysis, the ESD approach can help AAE speakers develop the metalinguistic awareness they need to monitor their use of AAE versus SWE. Moreover, ESD contrastive and error analyses can help teachers tailor instruction to their students' needs. The ESD approach may, however, bore students with drills and unintentionally send negative messages about AAE and SWE.

The Dialect Awareness Approach

As a supplement or alternative to an ESD approach, many sociolinguists have promoted dialect awareness programs in the schools, programs that "promote an understanding and appreciation for language variation" (Wolfram, "Repercussions" 62). For instance, in 1997 the American Association for Applied Linguistics passed a resolution that maintained that "all students and teachers should learn scientifically-based information about linguistic diversity" and that "education should systematically incorporate information about language variation." Among the foremost proponents of this approach is Wolfram. In fact, while advocating dialect education for everyone, he insists that "the most effective method for teaching Standard English would incorporate dialect awareness" (62).

Philosophy

The dialect awareness approach aims to realize the goals of pluralists, for it seeks to stamp out linguistic prejudice in society as a whole. Wolfram declares:

> There is an obvious need for knowledge about dialects for people at all levels of formal and informal education. Language variation affects us all, regardless of region, class, or ethnicity, and

dialect awareness programs seem to be the only way to counter the destructive social, educational, and political effects of misguided notions about this phenomenon. ("Repercussions" 62)

Central to the dialect awareness approach is the language attitude hypothesis. Advocates of dialect awareness programs target negative language attitudes because they believe such attitudes threaten the development of literacy as well as democracy. They contend that, prior to studying SWE, AAE speakers should feel positive about AAE. After all, if AAE speakers feel AAE stems from some intellectual or linguistic deficiency, why should they even try to master another language or dialect? At the same time, AAE speakers must feel positive about SWE. Otherwise, why should they bother to learn it?

Since AAE speakers' peers, family, and other community members shape those feelings, Wolfram and Schilling-Estes maintain that "the teaching of standard English must take into account the group reference factor" (288). Calling the group reference factor "the most essential of all the factors affecting the learning of Standard English," they contend that schools must "mold peer and indigenous community influence into a constructive force endorsing the standard variety" if they want students to master it (288). Ultimately, students must believe and reassure one another that Standard English can play a meaningful role in their lives (289).

Instruction

Because language attitudes play a critical role in the dialect awareness approach, instruction in Standard English must begin with a discussion of dialect differences. Bill Williams, a dialect awareness teacher, initiates such a discussion through the video *American Tongues* (Alvarez and Kolker), which exposes myths and prejudices about dialect differences.

After some discussion, Williams asks Jamal and his classmates to engage in scientific inquiry through inductive exercises that reveal how natural and rule governed dialects are. These exercises feature not only AAE but also other nonstandard dialects, and they reveal how the English language as a whole has evolved over the centuries. The students start with an exercise on the *a-* prefix in Appalachian English, a nonstandard dialect that is often derisively attributed to "hillbillies" in the Appalachian Mountain region. Using their intuition, the students examine pairs of sentences such as the following to determine which *-ing* words sound better with an *a-* prefix (Wolfram, "Repercussions" 68–71):

List A
1. a. Building is hard work.
   b. She was building a house.
2. a. The child was charming the adults.
   b. The child was very charming.

List B
1. a. She was discovering a trail.
   b. She was following a trail.
2. a. She was repeating the chant.
   b. She was hollering the chant.

By choosing the sentences that sound better with an *a-* prefix (see the boldface below), the students can inductively discover the rules that determine when a speaker can attach an *a-* to the beginning of an *-ing* word:

List A Rule: Attach the *a-* prefix to *-ing* words that act like verbs.
1. a. Building is hard work. (*Building* acts like a noun.)
   b. **She was a-building a house.**
2. a. **The child was a-charming the adults.**
   b. The child was very charming. (*Charming* acts like an adjective.)

List B Rule: Attach the *a-* prefix to a stressed syllable.
1. a. She was dis cov´ er ing a trail.
   b. **She was a-fol´ low ing a trail.**
2. a. She was re peat´ ing the chant.
   b. **She was a-hol´ ler ing the chant.**

After analyzing the *a-* prefix, the students complete an inductive exercise to discover a rule in AAE, such as the rule for using verbal *-s* (see the exercise in Appendix B). To complete certain exercises, Jamal's class might even collect data in their community (Wolfram, "Repercussions" 68).

When the students have shared their findings, Williams is ready to contrast African American and Standard English. He asks the students to discuss or act out scenarios that demonstrate the value of learning both. Although AAE proves to be the preferred medium in some scenarios, "the key here," Wolfram and Schilling-Estes explain, "is to stress that there may be immediate needs for standard English as well as the vernacular variety" (288–89).

Ideally, Williams would offer Standard English instruction only to students who feel they need it (Wolfram and Schilling-Estes 289). In accordance with parents' and administrators' expectations, however, Williams provides SWE instruction for the whole class. First, he engages the students in further contrastive analysis, but mainly in the context of their writing. For instance, if a peer editing session reveals that Jamal and his classmates are struggling with the third-person -s, Williams will teach a minilesson pinpointing the differences between AAE and SWE rules of subject-verb agreement (Wolfram, Adger, and Christian 137). To reinforce the lesson and develop metalinguistic awareness, Williams will also ask Jamal to note in his journal when the third-person -s does and does not occur in his speaking or writing (Adger). In any event, Williams will try to avoid assigning the contrastive drills that are the mainstay of many English as a Second Dialect programs.

Assessment

Williams advises his students to postpone editing so that they can focus their attention on content as they draft their essays. Therefore, when he reviews Jamal's first draft, he too focuses on content. Of course, as he reads he notices that the third-person -s is still a problem for Jamal as well as other students, so in class he reviews the AAE and SWE rules for subject-verb agreement. Then he reminds Jamal to look for subject-verb agreement problems before submitting the final draft.

When Williams reads Jamal's final draft, in addition to commenting on the content and organization, he points out patterns of SWE errors, including the frequent omission of the third-person -*s*. But since the omission is dialectal, he does not actually consider it an "error"; in fact, he refers to it as a "writing miscue" (Wolfram, Adger, and Christian 135). He prioritizes Jamal's miscues so that Jamal and he can focus on one or two at a time throughout the semester. Right now, since third-person subject-verb agreement is still Jamal's most frequent miscue, it (along with a recurring problem with paragraph development) will become the focus of Williams's comments, instruction, and grading (135–37).

As for testing, Williams relies solely on Jamal's school writing to assess his progress. He refuses to administer standardized multiple-choice or essay tests because he feels they target nonstandard dialects.

Research

LANGUAGE ATTITUDES

Williams's dialect awareness approach is supported by the same research on second language learning that supports the language attitude hypothesis (see Chapter 3). There is also some evidence that dialect awareness pedagogy changes students' language attitudes. For instance, citing an unpublished evaluation by K. Messner, Wolfram indicates that his dialect awareness activities have had a substantial impact on students' language attitudes ("Repercussions" 67). His colleague, Carolyn Temple Adger, also reports that "informal evaluation" of the program "indicates that students come to recognize that dialect contrasts occur regularly, rather than haphazardly, and they become aware that dialect prejudice is not justifiable."

More formal evaluations of the effects on students' attitudes are needed, however. Furthermore, empirical studies establishing a causal link between AAE speakers' attitudes and their SWE progress remain to be done. As for the effects of dialect awareness activities on SWE learning, while such activities play a part in some other pedagogical approaches, we have not found empirical studies of programs that rely wholly on this approach.

LINGUISTICALLY BIASED TESTS

Williams's suspicions about standardized testing are well founded. Edward White and Leon Thomas concluded that the College Board's Test of Standard Written English (TSWE) was biased against African Americans, Mexican Americans, and Asian Americans after they compared students' performance on the TSWE and California's English Placement Test. Wolfram, Adger, and Christian propose that such results reflect a linguistic bias because standardized tests target precisely those points where dialects differ. The tests also solicit choices or essays based on language experiences that many AAE speakers may have never had (138–39). As the next section of this chapter reveals, however, cultural bias may also play a role in testing.

To sum up, the dialect awareness approach can help *all* students develop positive attitudes about *all* language varieties, not just AAE or SWE. But we need more empirical evidence to document how increasing students' dialect awareness influences their progress in mastering SWE.

The Culturally Appropriate Approach

Although dialect awareness may play an important role in their pedagogy, some writing teachers focus on *cultural* awareness. In the case of AAE speakers, they adopt a curriculum and methodology that are steeped in African American culture. Known as "Afrocentric," "African-centered," "culturally relevant," or "culturally engaged" teaching, culturally appropriate teaching (CAT) draws on the knowledge, strategies, and experiences from African American students' culture.

With roots in the segregated black schools of the South (V. Walker 769–71), CAT reemerged during the Civil Rights/Black Power era. One of the pioneers was education professor Mary Hoover, who co-founded the Nairobi Day School in 1966. For eighteen years, the Nairobi Day School taught writing and other subjects by combining a basic skills approach with Afrocentric materials and strategies (Hoover, "Nairobi" 202). With the institutionalization of Black Studies in the 1970s, culturally appropriate teaching gained a foothold in college composition classes, where some teachers started letting students read and write about African American texts. Although English teachers began compiling anthologies of African American writing for composition students as early as 1931 (see Cromwell, Turner, and Dykes), after the 1970s such anthologies became more common (see recent examples such as Anokye and Brice-Finch's *Get It Together*; Lee, Jarrett, and Mbalia's *Heritage*; Redd's *Revelations*).

Philosophy

CAT responds to the call of Molefi Kete Asante, Asa Hilliard, Ivan Van Sertima, and other scholars to improve the education of African Americans by infusing the curriculum with an Afrocentric content (Hilliard, Payton-Stewart, and Williams). According to Asante, an Afrocentric curriculum portrays black people "as the subjects rather than the objects of education. . . . [I]t centers African American students inside history, culture, science, and so forth rather than outside these subjects" (171–72).

In the composition classroom, CAT centers students within African American traditions of literacy in the hopes of countering the cultural resistance to SWE that is predicted by the language attitude hypothesis. According to compositionist Thomas Fox, such positioning "requires a pedagogy that would investigate the ways in which history, culture, institutions, social relations, and race intersect and influence writing" (292). From their new position—firmly anchored in the African American tradition—African American students can connect themselves to academic SWE discourse without disconnecting themselves from their heritage (Richardson, *African* 97). As such, they can not only master SWE discourse but also critique and transform it to liberate themselves and their people. Thus, CAT promotes Paulo Freire's rhetoric of critical literacy.

Instruction

To see CAT in action, let's suppose that Latisha Jones is a CAT teacher. She grew up in the sort of community where most of her students grew up, so she understands their cultural values. In fact, while she models the use of Standard English, like the legendary African American preacher she speaks with the intonation, imagery, and rhythm of AAE and readily switches to AAE grammar or vocabulary to drive home a point. At times invoking the African American church ritual, she even engages students in call-response. Regardless of how she chooses to express herself, she communicates her high expectations for her students.

Hers is a literature-based composition course because she believes that readings by and about African Americans can inspire her students. As Fox observes, "African American literature . . . argues forcefully against the separation of school literacy from the traditions of African American writing, against the notion that learning to write is learning to be white" (300). Therefore, the semester opens with the reading of narratives by enslaved Africans such as Olaudah Equiano and Frederick Douglass. Through reading and discussing the narratives, Jones seeks to develop her students' critical reading skills, especially an appreciation of how African Americans have used writing to signify— "to critique the dominant culture's view of reality" (Richardson "Critique"). To help students connect their experience with that of the enslaved Africans, Jones helps them extrapolate from the texts recurring themes of the Black Experience, such as racism, assimilation, and, the most crucial theme, "literacy as freedom" (Richardson, "Critique").

Later, after Jones has introduced the students to the form of the academic essay, she asks them to compose an essay in response to the following prompt:

> Discuss the lives of any of the enslaved Africans: Gronnioswa, Equiano, Drumgoold, Kizzy, Kunte Kinte, Douglass. Connect their experience as an African in America to your own. (Richardson, "Critique")

Jones asks the students to prepare to read their drafts aloud so that they can perform for the group and profit from the group's reactions and suggestions. She encourages this sort of cooperative learning because group participation is typical of African and African American communication, as seen in the call-and-response mode (see Chapter 2). Group members will also help one another revise their drafts.

While revising, Jamal and his group members begin to focus on their problems with the SWE third-person -*s*, and so does Jones. She wants them to learn not only SWE but also as many languages as they can so that they can expand their repertoire of survival strategies (Hoover, "Culturally" 24). To ready them for this task, she discusses the rule-governed features of AAE and contrasts them with corresponding features of SWE. Throughout the discussion, she stresses that the students are heirs to a literate tradition dating back to the ancient Ethiopians, who created the first alphabet with vowels. Standard English is part of that tradition, she explains, and illustrates her point by reading aloud a speech by Martin Luther King, Jr. Pointing to King as a model, she encourages the students to wield Standard English as he did, combining SWE grammar with the rhetorical style that marks authors and speakers as black. This, she says, is **Black Standard English** (Lewis 191–95). It is in this context that Jamal and his classmates proofread their drafts for SWE subject-verb agreement.

Since Jamal's draft reveals a number of agreement problems, Jones assigns him extra homework. Knowing how much African American life moves to rhythm, she asks Jamal to find and recite a poem that repeats the third-person -*s* (Dandy 154–55) while addressing some aspect of the Black Experience (Hoover, "Nairobi" 207). Or she asks him to play Lyric Shuffle: First he must copy or transcribe the lyrics of a song he likes, choosing only lyrics that are rendered in Standard English. Then, before class, he must circle the verbal -*s* endings (or locate more suitable lyrics if there are none). During class he and his teammates will compete to construct new sentences that incorporate the third-person verbs from the lyrics while using the number of words determined by the roll of two dice. As they play the game, Jones will award the teams points according to the number of words in each sentence. At the end of class, the team with the most points will win (Baugh, *Out* 34–40).

When Jones finds that the third-person -*s* continues to pose problems for Jamal and his classmates, she develops a literature-based lesson on the -*s* ending. First she presents an African folktale that repeats the third-person -*s* (e.g., Arkhurst's "Why Spider Lives in Ceilings"), writing the title on the board and underlining the -s ending. After discussing the content of the folktale, she directs the students to jot down the words that had the third-person -s ending (as many as they can remember) along with the subjects. Then she asks the students to compose a different ending to the folktale, making sure they include several words with the third-person -s (Ball, "Language" 34). (See Appendix B for a higher-level literature-based exercise.)

Assessment

To encourage experimentation, Jones assesses SWE errors only in Jamal's final drafts, and when she does, she considers the AAE-related features not as errors or miscues "but as a matter of language choice" (Kamusikiri 198). As Kamusikiri explains, "All writers must make language choices appropriate to the audience, subject, and purpose of an essay. . . . When we adopt an Afrocentric approach, we recognize that AAE is one of those choices," a choice that is political as well as editorial (198–99).

To comprehend students' language choices, Jones relies on writing conferences. Conferences play a critical role in Jones's assessment of writers like Jamal who rely heavily on their oral resources. During a conference, Jamal can explain himself, using gestures, facial expressions, and intonation (Ball, "Evaluating" 241). At the same time, Jones can pose questions to clear up misunderstandings, including any cultural misinterpretations of the assigned task (Thompson 228). Once Jones understands what Jamal intended to say, she exclaims, "'Look what you have done here! Here are the things that are influenced by your own cultural patterns. Here are the things you did well, and here are some new features that I'd like to see you incorporate into your ever-broadening range of resources'" (Ball, "Evaluating" 244). As you can see, whether she responds face-to-face or in writing, Jones always couples her suggestions with positive feedback.

Jones does not feel positive about standardized testing, however, for she believes that the tests are culturally biased. That is why she conducts her own essay testing to supplement standardized testing if her school demands standardized test scores (Hoover, "Culturally" 25; Hoover and Politzer).

Research

The Role of Culture

Research affirms the major premise of the culturally appropriate approach, that culture plays an important role in the learning process for African Americans. Having identified "nine dimensions of Afrocultural expression," Wade Boykin found that African American students learned better when there were opportunities for rhythmic movement, varied stimulation, and group cooperation—three of the nine dimensions (249, 253–54). Moreover, as noted in Chapter 3, numerous studies of effective teachers of African American students suggest that these teachers are effective in part because they feel "connected" to their students' culture. Like Marva Collins, founder of the high-achieving Westside Prep school, they also enhance their teaching style with cultural communicative patterns such as call-and-response, metaphors, and rhythm (Foster 229–37).

CAT, however, raises questions of inclusiveness. For one, how can non–African American teachers adopt such an approach? English teacher Hafeezah AdamaDavia Dalji admits that it is not easy, though it is possible if they listen to their students during and after class (Meier 115). David Holmes, on the other hand, wonders how CAT serves the African American student who does not speak AAE (60). An Afrocentric curriculum does not exclude such students, from Richardson's perspective. AAE, she reminds us, is not just a matter of grammar and pronunciation. It is "a continuum from vernacular to standard forms," where many standard-speaking African Americans still engage in traditional AAE rhetorical practices (*African* 155).

Afrocentric Curriculum

So where is the evidence to support Afrocentric instruction? In 1990, Joan Ratteray despaired that there were not enough empirical studies to test the effectiveness of Afrocentric instruction and that the results of existing studies were inconclusive. Fortunately, since then the body of evidence has been growing.

For instance, there is some evidence that having students read and write about African American texts develops more positive attitudes toward writing. During the 1991–92 academic year, 911 of 1,305 first-year college students completed questionnaires about their Afrocentric composition textbook. The survey revealed the following:

- Ninety-four percent enjoyed reading about the Afrocentric issues, while 64 percent enjoyed writing about them.

- Eighty percent felt more positive about writing in general because they had read so many essays by black writers.

- Seventy-five percent thought they had something worthwhile to say when writing about the Afrocentric issues, while only 6 percent said they did not. (Redd, "Afrocentric" 5–9)

Afrocentric texts may also be an effective vehicle for teaching SWE grammar. When Arnetha Ball taught SWE grammar in the context of mainly African and African American literature, African American second graders significantly increased their use of the SWE linking verb *be*, plural -*s*, and possessive ("Language" 34, 41). (All of the testing, however, was oral.)

Other scholars have reported success in using African American musical practices (such as rap) or readings *about* the music as a "scaffolding" to move students toward SWE mastery (e.g., Gilmore; Mahiri).[1] For instance, Noma LeMoine has combined African American literature and music to teach language arts to African American children. Also, although Los Angeles's Academic English Mastery Program draws heavily on ESD methodology, LeMoine's Afrocentric strategies may have contributed to the success rate cited earlier in this chapter.

The most persuasive evidence supporting an Afrocentric composition curriculum, however, comes from Diane Pollard and Cheryl Ajirotutu's and Elaine Richardson's studies. Pollard and Ajirotutu report significant gains in writing as well as reading and math for students at Milwaukee's Martin Luther King, Jr. elementary school six years after the school became an African immersion school. They attribute the gains largely to the African-centered education, although increased support from the community and school district may have contributed as well.

Richardson, in turn, evaluates an Afrocentric course that she taught at a Big Ten university. Her literature-based course focused on the language and literacy tradition of African Americans. Through readings, discussions, movies, and music as well as contrastive analysis, students explored AAE grammar and rhetoric along with SWE. Although there was no control group, an in-group comparison revealed that students who incorporated more AAE rhetoric wrote longer and better essays (as measured by holistic raters). A pretest-posttest comparison also revealed at least a 10 percent decrease in the omission of the *-ed* and *-s* endings and a 6 percent decrease in the omission of the linking verb *be*. Like Smitherman (*Talkin That Talk* 183), Richardson also found that the more AAE rhetorical features students incorporated, the less AAE grammar they used. Noting this trend, Richardson speculates, "conscious usage of Black discourse features may have the effect of making students more careful in their writing, not less" (*African* 104).

CULTURALLY BIASED TESTING

Research bolsters Jones's claims about cultural bias in standardized testing. As Liz Hamp-Lyons observes, cultural bias in standardized multiple-choice exams is well documented "because of culture-specific or culturally offensive content or test takers' unfamiliarity with testing practices" (51). Cultural bias in essay testing is becoming more and more apparent. Mary Hoover, Robert Politzer, Miriam Chaplin, Roscoe Brown, Dorothy Perry Thompson, and others have shown that the wording, formats, choices, topics, and scoring criteria for writing tests often tap cultural knowledge that is unavailable to many African American students, especially those from poor, segregated neighborhoods. For instance, Thompson recalls how two AAE speakers misinterpreted the word *pollster* as a first name in an essay prompt that read "'Pollster Daniel Yankelovich estimated. . . .'" (228). "To these students," Thompson explains, "Pollster, as a first name, is no more unusual than Yankelovich as a last name. Moreover, neither student had ever heard of pollster as an occupation identifier" (228).

To sum up, the CAT approach can help teachers motivate AAE speakers to learn SWE by positioning the students in the African American tradition of literacy. It can also facilitate the mastery of the standard by teaching SWE skills via AAE communicative patterns, such as music and call-response. Though the body of evidence supporting CAT is limited, it is steadily growing.

The Bridge Approach

The last of our five approaches, the bridge approach, originated in bilingual education. Since the 1950s, international studies have shown that students who study school subjects in their native language before being taught in a second language quickly catch up with—or surpass—students who began their studies in a second language (Rickford, *AAVE* 340–41). In the 1970s, Gary Simpkins, Grace Holt, and Charlesetta Simpkins adapted this approach to reading instruction for AAE speakers by developing a series of textbooks called Bridge readers. Published by Houghton Mifflin, these books attempted to "bridge" the gap between AAE and SWE by teaching AAE speakers to read books written in AAE, then books written in a mixture of AAE and SWE, and, finally, books written in just SWE. Predictably, because of the initial focus on AAE, the series evoked such negative reactions from the public (including African American parents) that Houghton Mifflin stopped publishing the series (Rickford, "Language" 19–20). Despite Houghton Mifflin's decision, however, the Bridge concept did not die. In fact, it has reemerged in composition pedagogy, where the goal is to teach AAE speakers to write SWE by allowing them to write their early drafts (and sometimes certain finished pieces) in AAE.

Philosophy

The rationale for the bridge approach is simple: to "present AAVE speakers with the same initial task as that of SE speakers, [in this case learning to write] without confronting them with the additional task of acquiring SE at the same time" (Rickford, "Language" 20). Here we can see the impact of the composing process hypothesis, for the bridge approach assumes that many AAE speakers fail to "edit out" AAE features in their essays because they are trying to juggle other composing tasks (e.g., formulating a thesis, synthesizing information, and structuring paragraphs). That is why composition theorist Peter Elbow tells his students, "Experiment to see whether it isn't easier to achieve SWE at the very end when you can give your full attention to it and you have no other tasks to distract you" (133).

On the other hand, education specialist Henry Evans justifies the bridge approach as a way to affirm the more "holistic" style of AAE rhetoric versus the "analytical" style of Western rhetoric. He explains, "This approach shows African American students that they do not have to see the components of the [Afrocentric] holistic worldview in their writing as nonacademic or in error; they come to recognize worldview differences and the sociopolitical implications of each in education and in United States society" (279). Evans even encourages students to transform academic discourse by mixing, for instance, SWE grammar and Afrocentric terms (e.g., *endarkening* instead of *enlightening*) (281).

By inviting AAE speakers to invent **alternative rhetorics,** Evans seeks to defuse the resistance anticipated by the language attitude hypothesis. So does Kermit Campbell. That is why he recommends that students use AAE to write personal narratives that signify on mainstream academic culture. In this way, he argues, teachers can "equip them to compose rather than be composed," to affirm themselves and their community in the face of the dominant culture ("The *Signifying*"). Both he and Troutman contend that AAE speakers need such opportunities so that they can develop the sense of authority required for academic writing tasks (Troutman, "Whose Voice" 38; Campbell, "Real Niggaz" 69).

Instruction

Consider how Malcolm Smith applies this approach in Jamal's classroom. He begins by distributing an excerpt from Alice Walker's *The Color Purple* to prove that some of today's most popular authors write in AAE. Citing the works of Dante and Chaucer, he explains that even some of the Western "classics" were written in oral dialects that were considered at the time to be unfit for writing. Therefore, he announces that for his course all of the students' finished pieces need not conform to SWE grammar and rhetoric—only four of the six main papers (Elbow 130–31, 135). Smith also announces that he will assign several African American autobiographies that incorporate AAE, books by H. Rap Brown, Claude Brown, Malcolm X, and Zora Neale Hurston. As the students read these books, he wants them to act like ethnographers, commenting in their journals on the authors' use of language (Campbell, "Real Niggaz" 77).

After discussing his pluralistic philosophy, Smith asks the students to freewrite on a topic:

> Try to use this freewriting for whatever language comes most easily and naturally to your mouth and ear—that feels most comfortable, most yours. If it's different from school language or formal writing, that doesn't make it wrong. Do you remember the powerful published writing we read together—where eminent authors used various home dialects of English? (Elbow 130–31).

Initially, Smith has students freewrite in their journals in class. Then he directs them to compose and post first drafts online, where the class listserv or discussion board becomes a "safe house" for AAE (Canagarajah 180; Redd, "Tryin").

This linguistic freedom extends to classroom discussion and the rhetorical mode of the students' writing as well—even if Smith expects the final product in SWE. Although Smith may ultimately want students to produce a fairly impersonal, thesis-driven causal analysis or research paper, he permits them to begin where they are most comfortable, such as with the storytelling mode that is so strong in AAE rhetoric (Campbell, "Real Niggaz" 76; Wang). Or he invites them to write from an AAE field-dependent perspective, addressing their readers as "you" throughout an academic argument (Evans 279).

Then Smith pushes the students to "rewrite, revise; rewrite, revise; rewrite, revise; and once they have produced the most powerful essay possible, then and only then [does he] have them turn their attention to [SWE] grammar and matters of punctuation, spelling, and mechanics" (Smitherman, *Talkin That Talk* 186). Midway during the revision process, Smith asks students to find the major points embedded in the most recent draft and to make sure that the next draft presents these (and, if necessary, other points) in a hierarchical and less personal manner (Elbow 134).

A couple of drafts later, Smith requests the "final final draft or copyedited draft" (Elbow 132). To prepare the students for copyediting, he conducts a fifteen-minute miniworkshop on the SWE third-person *-s* because he has noticed that Jamal and several other classmates usually omit it. During the workshop, he contrasts the SWE and AAE rules for subject-verb agreement. Then he encourages the class to keep this contrast in mind as they copyedit their drafts (132). (See the sample instructions in Appendix B.)

Assessment

When Smith responds to Jamal's early drafts, he strives to "read *through* grammar and syntax to the content" (Elbow 132). Consequently, he passes over the frequent omissions of third-person *-s* as well as other SWE errors. Instead, he focuses his comments on ideas, reasoning, organization, and clarity. Only when he reads the penultimate draft does he offer feedback on grammar. He hopes that now there will be far fewer SWE errors since Jamal should not have been distracted by concerns about content or organization. If SWE errors remain on the first page or within a paragraph, however, Smith will circle them. If it is the first month of classes, he may even write a comment suggesting a correction (133). After Smith returns the paper, Jamal will correct it and add this "final final draft" to his portfolio for grading.

As for standardized testing, Smith dismisses conventional multiple-choice and essay tests as linguistically and culturally biased. Instead, he insists on portfolio assessment because it can embrace both traditional and nontraditional writing, including experimental writing that blends AAE and SWE (e.g., academic prose interspersed with narration or an essay that code-switches to satirize SWE). But Smith does not consider portfolio assessment to be bias-free either. He suspects that in a department-wide portfolio assessment the standards for scoring would be biased toward SWE rhetoric, grammar, spelling, and mechanics (Mountford 386–87).

Research

COMPOSING IN AAE

Smith derives his strategies from research on the composing process, which suggests that writers perform better when they divide composing into subtasks such as generating ideas, organizing, revising, and proofreading (Flower and Hayes 41). Since writing in SWE requires a lot of an AAE speaker's attention, we would expect students who write initially in AAE and rewrite in SWE to perform better than those who write in SWE only. Unfortunately, as far as we know, there are no empirical tests of this approach to writing, and several studies of the approach to reading have yielded nonsignificant results (McWhorter, *Word* 220).

A large-scale study of Bridge reading instruction, however, suggests that a similar approach might succeed in writing. When Simpkins and Simpkins tested their Bridge readers with 417 students in twenty-one classes across the United States, they found that in four months the Bridge students had gained 6.2 months on the Iowa Test of Basic Skills, while the control groups in conventional reading programs had gained only 1.6 months. John Rickford speculates that this study uncovered such dramatic gains because the instruction lasted for four months, whereas the other studies introduced Bridge readers "at one point in time" ("Language" 19–21). On the other hand, since the Simpkins' Bridge readers consisted of African and African American stories, the appeal of the Afrocentric content (Rickford, "Language" 24) and the literature-based instruction (Van Keulen, Weddington, and DeBose 199) may have also contributed to the success of the program.

ALTERNATIVE RHETORICS

As for his endorsement of alternative rhetorics, history certainly vindicates Smith. After all, in the Middle Ages, Latin reigned as the only literate tongue, while English, French, Italian, and Spanish were stigmatized as the speech of the common people. "And now?" Elbow remarks, "Latin has virtually disappeared. The upstart, oral, low vernaculars are now official literacies" (127). We can see that process continuing today as Geneva Smitherman,

Keith Gilyard, and Elaine Richardson publish—with much ac-claim—academic discourse that includes AAE rhetoric and even AAE grammar.

PORTFOLIO ASSESSMENT

Considering the research on assessment, there is good reason for Smith to rely on portfolios. Research suggests that, compared to multiple-choice or timed essay tests, portfolio assessment may be a fairer and more accurate measure of nonmainstream students' writing because the students have a chance to clarify the instruc-tional and social context for their writing—particularly the teacher's expectations regarding the appropriate audience, pur-pose, and discourse mode. Moreover, since portfolios can con-tain multiple writing samples on different subjects for different purposes and different audiences, teachers can assess AAE speak-ers' overall language use, especially their code-switching ability (Kamusikiri 201–2).

To sum up, the bridge approach might help students better manipulate SWE by allowing them to focus on SWE only at the end of their composing process. By endorsing alternative rheto-rics and a multilingual portfolio assessment, the approach also promotes greater equity. It deserves to be empirically tested.

Summary

The five approaches described in this chapter offer writing teach-ers conflicting choices. While, for example, the traditional ap-proach replaces AAE with Standard English (both spoken and written), the bridge approach not only adopts AAE as scaffold-ing to learn SWE but also encourages students to transform aca-demic discourse. Whereas the traditional and second dialect approaches rely heavily on grammar drills, the dialect awareness and bridge approaches shun them.

So what should a writing teacher do?

First, teachers should look for commonalities. The second dialect, dialect awareness, culturally appropriate, and bridge ap-proaches are not as different as they may at first look. All promote explicit teaching of the contrasts between AAE and SWE features to develop students' metalinguistic awareness. All acknowledge culture as an important factor in students' learning. And all invite the use of AAE in some form in the classroom or curriculum.

While following these common principles, teachers should be eclectic in their choice of methods. Research suggests there is no one-size-fits-all pedagogy for teaching AAE speakers Standard Written English. Despite their common heritage, AAE speakers bring diverse learning styles, attitudes, socioeconomic backgrounds, and personal experiences into the classroom. Age differences may also affect how readily students acquire AAE. So different strokes will work for different folks. Moreover, different strategies seem to work for different features. Recall that Ball's traditional approach helped students learn the third-person -s, while her culturally appropriate approach helped them learn the SWE possessive. No wonder most of the successful programs cited in this chapter combined strategies. Clearly, the research invites us to combine and alternate, appropriating the most appropriate method for a particular assignment or student.

Note

1. It is worth noting that Carol Lee, who popularized the term *scaffolding,* used signifyin to teach students literary terms such as *metaphor* and *irony.* Her success suggests that other teachers might tap signifyin and other AAE rhetorical practices to teach SWE grammar in composition classes.

Suggested Readings

Adger, Carolyn Temple, Donna Christian, and Orlando L. Taylor. *Making the Connection: Language and Academic Achievement among African American Students.* Washington, DC: Center for Applied Linguistics, 1999.

Brooks, Charlotte K., ed. *Tapping Potential: English and Language Arts for the Black Learner.* Urbana, IL: National Council of Teachers of English, 1985.

Clinton Crawford, ed. *Ebonics and Language Education of African Ancestry Students*. New York: Sankofa, 2001.

Dandy, Evelyn Baker. *Black Communications: Breaking Down the Barriers*. Chicago: African American Images, 1991.

Delpit, Lisa, and Joanne Kilgour Dowdy, eds. *The Skin That We Speak: Thoughts on Language and Culture in the Classroom*. New York: New Press, 2002.

Farr, Marcia, and Harvey Daniels. *Language Diversity and Writing Instruction*. Urbana, IL: ERIC Clearinghouse on Reading and Communication Skills, 1986.

Mahiri, Jabari. *Shooting for Excellence: African American and Youth Culture in New Century Schools*. Urbana, IL, and New York: National Council of Teachers of English and Teachers College Press, 1998.

McWhorter, John. *Spreading the Word: Language and Dialect in America*. Portsmouth, NH: Heinemann, 2000.

Reed, Carol E. "Adapting TESL Approaches to the Teaching of Written Standard English as a Second Dialect to Speakers of American Black English Vernacular." *TESOL Quarterly* 7 (1973): 289–307.

Richardson, Elaine. *African American Literacies*. London: Routledge, 2003.

Schroeder, Christopher, Helen Fox, and Patricia Bizzell, eds. *ALT DIS: Alternative Discourses and the Academy*. Portsmouth, NH: Boynton/Cook, Heinemann, 2002.

Severino, Carol, Juan C. Guerra, and Johnnella E. Butler, eds. *Writing in Multicultural Settings*. New York: Modern Language Association, 1997.

Smitherman, Geneva. *Talkin That Talk: Language, Culture, and Education in African America*. London: Routledge, 2000.

Smitherman, Geneva, and Victor Villanueva, eds. *Language Diversity in the Classroom: From Intention to Practice*. Carbondale: Southern Illinois UP, 2003.

Taylor, Hanni U. *Standard English, Black English, and Bidialectalism: A Controversy*. New York: P. Lang, 1989.

Whiteman, Marcia Farr, ed. *Variation in Writing: Functional and Linguistic-Cultural Differences*. Hillsdale, NJ: Lawrence Erlbaum, 1981.

Wolfram, Walter. Carolyn Temple Adger, and Donna Christian. *Dialects in Schools and Communities*. Mahwah, NJ: Lawrence Erlbaum, 1999.

Conclusion

As I tell my bright, eager, committed-to-making-a-difference students, they don't need to know anything about Ebonics to become teachers. They only need that knowledge if they want to become great *teachers.*

Terry Meier

As Terry Meier states, one of the differences between good teachers and great teachers is what great teachers know about their students' language use. Great teachers make it their business to find out what kind of language competence their students bring into the classroom. We have seen from Chapters 1 and 2 the verbal competence of many AAE speakers. We have seen the ingenuity of their vocabulary, the economy of their pronunciation, the complexity of their grammar, and the power of their rhetoric.

As successful writers, we have learned strategies that normally allow us to match our competence to the required performance level. How do we teach AAE speakers to do the same? Or, as it is popular to say nowadays, "How do you get there from here?" How can we assess these students' communicative competence (the "here"), teach the strategies needed, and help the students achieve the desired writing performance (the "there")?

The challenge for composition teachers is to add written communication strategies to our students' repertoire and assist them in formulating strategies for applying this knowledge to their writing. Essentially, they come to us with a set of literacy competencies, in addition to their rich oral language traditions, which they can apply to their academic writing. If their written performance is not congruent with the composition curriculum, however, then we need to build on the language competence that is in place, add to their language logic, make them aware of the writing strategies they are using, and give them the tools with which to transfer their knowledge to their written performance. We also need to explore ways to expand the composition curriculum to tap the rich, oral database our students bring with them.

When delineated, this process may seem daunting, especially as you consider the conflicting hypotheses in Chapter 3. But M. A. K. Halliday's structural analyses show that "oral language is, contrary to what most people think, at least as complex or 'grammatically intricate' as written language" (Hatch 246). Therefore, regardless of whether students speak African American or Standard English, their communicative competence is a strong foundation on which instructional strategies can be built. Chapter 4 shows how several teachers, working within different paradigms, attempt to build on this competence. We hope that this book has inspired you to do so.

Appendix A: Student Writing Samples and Analyses

Writing Samples

Pronunciation and Grammar

The following excerpts are drawn from African American first-year college students' essays, written for an introductory expository writing course. Interviews confirm that the authors are AAE speakers. All of the excerpts contain SWE errors—features that violate the rules of Standard Written English. Only a few of these features, however, conform to AAE rules. Using the information in Chapter 2 as a guide, identify the features that appear to be related to AAE and then check the analyses at the end of this appendix.

Sample 1
When entering a university or college, most students parents put a word or two into their child ear. If the student listen, its on him or her. But the advice your parents usually give you is right. Most students are introduce to drugs and alcohle and is put with the delima should they use it. Then start to think back at what they parent told them. They let it float in one ear and out the other.

Sample 2
Big Blow Out Sale! Final Sale! Save 50% of entire store! Shop at Priceline.com for the lowest prices. Today that is pretty much all you see on television. Every channel was some advertisement about either shopping online or going to your local mall for a big blow out sale. To many people the mall is a disaster area that should never been seen. To other the mall is a haven, a chance to meet new people and get hands on sales associate. With the invention of computer and the internet been so powerful, online shopping has become the norm for many customer. These two shopping techniques can have their advantages and disadvantages.

Sample 3
As the showed end for that week my friends and I were preparing to leave, but stop to socialize like everyoneelse was doing. For some strange reason we were singled out. "Gentlemen, cross the street", yelled the officer. We kept talking because we didn't know if he was referring to us. "Get off the property and cross the street", yelled the officer. So, I turned around and gestured to my friends lets leave and as we were crossing the street me friend Theron (Chocolate) got snatched up by an officer for no reason. The officer grabbed Choc threw him up against a car and twisted his arm behind his back for no reason. Choc ask what did he do and he said, "Shut up, your getting arrested tonight", and handcuffed him. Naturally, as friends we tried to help; in all the comotion my friend Chris got hancuffed also. So, they took Choc and Chris back inside the building.

Sample 4
Finally, If a child is not in the home or school, the community must serve as a rearing force. "It take a village, to rage a child" (African proverb) , is correct. It also take a village to stop violence in community. These two thoughts will make the community a safe place to live. Neighbors should pay attention to the behavior of children in the community. If they see children misbehaving, don't be afraid to tell the child's parents. That same child could be the future drug dealer that destroys the community even more. Communities should also ban together to stop crimes. Programs such as neighborhood watch has reduce crimes by 30% in the Crenshaw Blv. Area (Compton, CA). Awareness is the key to reduce violence. Along with watching children, neighbors should also watch property. Keep an eye out for crime decreases the chance of it happening.

Vocabulary and Rhetoric

The following passages, which are also taken from African American first-year college students' essays, illustrate some of the strategies that characterize AAE rhetoric. Using the information in Chapter 2, identify the AAE rhetorical devices and then check the analyses at the end of this appendix.

Sample 5
We will never be free to be until we achieve the kind of freedom that does not make it easier to criticize than it is to contribute. We will never be free to be until we achieve the kind of freedom that does not make the rich even richer while the poor become poorer.

We will never be free to be until we achieve the kind of freedom that encourages children to dream big things that may be difficult (but not impossible) to attain instead of small endeavors that pose no challenge. We will never be free to be until we achieve the kind of freedom that allows us to celebrate our history while looking to a better future. We will never be free to be until we achieve the kind of freedom that urges us to support one another in a united cause as opposed to everyone "doing their own thing." Only then will we be truly free to dream, free to make our dreams a reality, and simply free to be.

Sample 6
We are poor because we have been raped repeatedly. Doors are not opened to us, it has been a façade. We are poor not only economically but socially as well. We attempt as a people to climb from this hole, but dirt is constantly being piled on top of us, pushing us farther into our holes of despair.

Sample 7
The Afro-American feels that he must meet the status quo and were Gucci, Liz Claiborne, and Polo because those are the most expensive tastes of clothing, everyone wants to have the best. However, there's a problem when one does not have a phone or electricity due to that leather coat. Due to mixed up priorities, one better sleep in that leather coat to keep warm without electricity. Afro-Americans spend their money on the wrong things and so they suffer. Afro Americans are too materialistic instead of being realistic.

Sample 8
A great philosopher once said for every one door that closes, there are at least ten waiting to be broken down. Behind these doors lies the key from any hope and good life can be obtained. The road is going to be hard but any worth having is worth fighting for and the end result will be a race is worthy of it's culture.

Sample 9
More than anything, the messages that society bombards us with can be obstacles that can stigmatize and stunt independent thinking and beliefs. Think of the many authors who have written on this very situation. *The Bluest Eye* by writer Toni Morrison describes a situation with a black girl desiring to have the features of her white peers—eyes the same color as the day sky. Where did this desire spring from other than a society that taught her the importance of white beauty. Another writer, journalist Clarisse Jones, describes a stigma that has been instilled in many black children,

which subsequently they carry with them into adulthood—the ug-
liness of black skin and the beauty of "light skin, green eyes, and
long, wavy hair" (250). It will be hard to defeat a thought that is so
a part of the Black woman's thinking since a young age, as though
it were a part of her genes. However difficult or not, in order to
move to the second part of the twofold process of discovery of
beauty, the Black woman must have a clean palate on which to
taste their new found beauty.

Analyses of Writing Samples

Pronunciation and Grammar

SAMPLE 1

The author of this paragraph follows AAE rules for possession,
the passive voice, subject-verb agreement, pronunciation, and
questions:

- To indicate possession, the student juxtaposes *students* and *parents*, *child* and *ear*, and *they* and *parent*.

- To construct the passive, he uses the verb *introduce* without the standard *-ed* ending after the helping verb *are*.

- Meanwhile, he uses the verb stem *listen* with the subject *student* without the standard *-s* ending to mark the third-person singular in the present tense. (Notice, however, that the other subject-verb agreement error, *Most students . . . is put*, has more to do with the distance between the subject and the second verb than with AAE.)

- AAE pronunciation may have shaped this student's spelling of *dilemma* and *alcohol*. Many unskilled spellers might write *de* instead of *di* in *dilemma*. But since AAE speakers often pronounce *em* as *im*, *delima* appears to be an AAE-related spelling. Likewise, the AAE tendency to omit unstressed syllables may have contracted *alcohol* into *alcohle*.

- Finally, following the AAE rule, the student inverts the helping verb *should* and its subject *they* when SWE would have required an indirect question.

SAMPLE 2

You can see the influence of AAE on the perfective verb forms and plural nouns in this passage:

- For the perfective, the student author uses unstressed *been* without *have* in *should never been seen* and without *having* in *been so powerful*.

- He also omits the plural *-s* ending on *other* and *customer* where the context makes the number clear. Although he may have carelessly omitted the articles *a* and *the*, *associate* and *computer* appear to be AAE-derived plurals as well.

SAMPLE 3

Here we see hypercorrection as well as adherence to AAE rules for the past tense, questions, and subordinate clauses:

- Having been warned about missing *-ed* endings in a previous paper, the student mistakenly adds *-ed* to the noun *show* at the same time that he omits *-ed* on the past-tense verbs *end*, *stop*, and *ask*.

- He also constructs a direct question (*what did he do*) where SWE would insert a direct one. Likewise, he gives a direct command (*lets leave*) where SWE would attach a subordinate *that* clause (*that we should leave*) or infinitive phrase (*to leave*). (Note that the missing apostrophe in *lets* is unrelated to AAE grammar.)

- Although the missing *d* in *hancuffed* is consistent with AAE pronunciation, this misspelling is probably a typo (like *croos* and *me friend*) since *handcuffed* is spelled correctly in the preceding sentence.

SAMPLE 4

This excerpt illustrates AAE rules governing subject-verb agreement, pronunciation, the perfective, and topic-comment structure.

- Although its subject is *it*, the verb *take* lacks the standard *-s* ending that signals the third-person singular present tense.

- ◆ Like many AAE speakers, the student omits the final consonant in *band.*

- ◆ AAE can account for the missing *-ed* ending in the perfective phrase *has reduce.* The subject-verb disagreement between *programs* and *has,* however, is probably due to the intervening phrase *such as neighborhood watch.*

- ◆ This paragraph also contains shifts to the imperative (*don't be afraid to tell the child's parents* and *Keep an eye out for crime*) that may be related to AAE topic-comment structure and the student's attempt to master the rules of SWE.

- ◆ *Rage* appears to be an aural spelling—that is, what the writer heard when someone repeated the proverb.

Vocabulary and Rhetoric

SAMPLE 5

The musical and sermonic quality of this passage is obvious in the repetition of *We will never be free to be until we achieve the kind of freedom* and in the concluding line. Also evident are instances of wordplay, including antithesis (e.g., *big* versus *small*) and alliteration (e.g., *criticize* and *contribute*). Notice as well the allusion to the proverb "The rich get richer while the poor get poorer" and the conscious switch to AAE vocabulary in *doing their own thing.*

SAMPLE 6

This excerpt is rich in imagery and repetition. The student writer contrasts *doors* and *façade* and invokes an image of physical violence through the verb *raped.* Also, quite literally, she employs down-to-earth imagery to convey her people's despair (see *We attempt as a people to climb from this hole. . . .*).

SAMPLE 7

Both rhyme (*materialistic* and *realistic*) and admonition (*one better sleep in that leather coat*) give this excerpt an AAE flavor. The student writes with the directness of the AAE speaker who scoffs, "You better sleep in that leather coat!" but she tries to mimic the formal, elaborated style of academic prose by adding *due to*, *one*, and *to keep warm without electricity.*

SAMPLE 8

Every line of this passage is filled with proverbs, giving the prose its sermonic tone and everyday imagery.

SAMPLE 9

In many ways, this student adopts the vocabulary, syntax, and research conventions of the SWE academic essay. True to the AAE tradition, however, the student still expresses herself through close-to-home images such as *the day sky* and *a clean palate*, and she drives home her point through alliterative wordplay (*stigmatize and stunt*). In addition, taking a field-dependent approach, she seeks to become involved with her readers by giving them directions (*Think of the many authors. . . .*) and by asking them questions (*Where did this desire spring from. . . ?*).

Appendix B: Sample Assignments

The following assignments represent the five approaches described in Chapter 4. Each assignment attempts to teach students the same feature that is highlighted in the chapter: the verbal -*s* ending. Also, each assignment is modeled after published material that has been used in the classroom.

Traditional

(Model: an exercise in Whitten, Horner, and Webb's *Harbrace College Handbook*, 11th ed., 67)
Directions: Select the appropriate verb form within parentheses in each of the following sentences. Make sure each verb agrees with its subject according to the rules of Standard English.

1. That company (have, has) an ingenious solution.
2. Study habits (varies, vary) dramatically.
3. This computer (store, stores) thousands of names and addresses.
4. (Does, do) that speaker look familiar?
5. Children (need, needs) guidance and support from both parents.
6. A dictionary (provides, provide) more than definitions.
7. Several cars (is, are) speeding in a 35 mph zone.
8. Professor Newman (announce, announces) the homework at the beginning of each class.
9. Hard work (deserves, deserve) recognition.
10. Technology (change, changes) constantly.

Second Dialect

(Model: Hanni Taylor's lessons for college students in *Standard English, Black English, and Bidialectalism*, 112–13)
Directions: Read the paired sentences and circle the words that differ.

1. Reggie likes to drive his car on the highway.
   Reggie like to drive his car on the highway.

2. My neighborhood is predominantly black.
   My neighborhood are predominantly black.

3. She feels happy at home, not here.
   She feel happy at home, not here.

4. That girl come from Jamaica.
   That girl comes from Jamaica.

5. The student discusses poems by Langston Hughes.
   The student discuss poems by Langston Hughes.

6. Reverend Green preaches this Sunday.
   Reverend Green preach this Sunday.

7. My father loves jazz.
   My father love jazz.

8. Miguel speaks Spanish and English fluently.
   Miguel speak Spanish and English fluently.

9. The No. 14 bus stop here.
   The No. 14 bus stops here.

Dialect Awareness

(Model: a middle school lesson by Wolfram, Adger, and Christian 198–99; Green, 36–38, 99–102)
Directions: Let's look at verbs in African American English (AAE), a dialect spoken by many African Americans. Speakers of AAE usually omit the verbal *-s* ending in the present tense, but sometimes they include it. See if you can figure out the pattern.

1. First, study the following set of sentences:

I eat.	I run.	I move.
You eat.	You run.	You move.
He eat.	She run.	It move.
We eat.	We run.	We move.
They eat.	They run.	They move.

How does subject-verb agreement in African American English differ from subject-verb agreement in Standard English? How can listeners determine whether the verbs in African American English are singular or plural?

2. The preceding table shows you when AAE speakers omit the verbal -*s*. To understand when they may add it, take a look at the following sentences:

   a. When I think about Christmas, I gets excited.

   b. I sits and cries every night.

   c. Through thick and thin, the Lord haves us in his hands.

   Is the action completed or repeated? What, then, is the function of the verbal -*s* ending?

3. Now look at these passages:

   a. She had called me that night and said, "Come over here right away!" So I gets dressed, jumps in the car, and drives right over there.

   b. Last night the police yelled at me. I keeps walking because I knows I didn't do nothing. Then they gets outa the car and yells at me again. So I stops and stands real still.

   Both of these passages tell a story. So what else can you say about the use of the verbal -*s* ending in AAE?

4. Consider one more pattern:

   a. I loves my baby.

   b. Gots to be more careful!

   c. I wants to win.

Why do AAE speakers add *-s* to these verbs? If you know why, restate the verbal *-s* rule so that it takes into account all three *optional* uses of the verbal -s that you've just seen.

5. Now that you know when you can use the verbal *-s* in AAE, decide which sentences follow the rule. Write Y(es) if a sentence follows the AAE rule and N(o) if it doesn't.

   a. ___ My mother work at the Chrysler factory today.

   b. ___ Every time I hear her big mouth, I gets angry.

   c. ___ The teacher writes the formula on the board.

   d. ___ After the party, I drives home, takes a shower, and goes to sleep when all of a sudden . . .

   e. ___ He knows the truth now.

   f. ___ I needs this job.

Culturally Appropriate

(Model: a high school lesson by Hafeezah Adama Davia Dalji in Meier 113)
Directions:

1. Read the following excerpt from Malcolm X's speech "Message to the Grassroots":

   > This modern house Negro loves his master. He wants to live near him. He'll pay three times as much as the house is worth just to live near his master, and then brag about "I'm the only Negro out here." "I'm the only one on my job." "I'm the only one in this school." You're nothing but a house Negro. And if someone comes to you right now and says, "Let's separate," you say the same thing that the house Negro said on the plantation. "What you mean, separate? From America, this good white man? Where you going to get a better job than you get here?" I mean, this is what you say, "I ain't left nothing in Africa," that's what you say. Why, you left your mind in Africa.

2. What do you think of Malcolm's message in this passage? Write your reactions in your reading log.

3. When you have completed your entry, review the subject-verb agreement section of your grammar handbook, paying particular attention to the use of the -*s* ending with present-tense verbs in Standard English.

4. Then reread Malcolm's paragraph. Where does he add an -*s* ending to a verb? (List the verbs and their subjects.) In your own words, state the rule that he is following. Why do you think he follows Standard English rules in these instances but not in the dialogue?

5. Now return to your reading log. Have *you* followed the rule? Why or why not? If not, edit your entry so that—like Malcolm— you follow the rule.

Bridge

(Model: instruction described by Elbow 130–34)
Directions:

1. Freewrite about your topic in whatever language feels comfortable. If it doesn't look like school writing, that's okay.

2. Now cull the best ideas from your freewriting to compose a more organized and coherent first draft. But use the language you prefer. Post your draft on the class discussion board.

3. Comment on the ideas in your classmates' drafts and then read the comments on yours. Revise again. Submit the revision to me.

4. Review my comments on your content and organization and revise again until you've produced the most powerful message you can. Submit this revision to me.

5. Take notes during our Standard English workshop and review those notes before you copyedit the draft I return to you. When I return the draft, pay special attention to the words I have circled or the sentences I have underlined (e.g., subject-verb agreement problems). Keep in mind that the circled and underlined language does not conform to the rules of Standard English.

6. Decide whether Standard English is the most appropriate means to reach your target audience. If so, explain why and copyedit your paper to make sure it follows the rules of Standard English. If not, submit your paper as is, along with an explanation.

Appendix C:
Selected Web Sites

Amended Oakland Resolution of the Board of Education. The LIN-
GUIST List/The City of Oakland School Board. 26 Apr. 2004 <http:/
/linguistlist.org/topics/ebonics/ebonics-res2.html>.

Choy, Ron. *American Cultures: The Ebonics Controversy, Faculty Perspectives.* 27 Aug. 1997. University of California at Berkeley. 26
Apr. 2004 <http://ist-socrates.berkeley.edu/~jour200/biobibdocs/>.

Discussions about Ebonics: The American Dialect Society Debate. 20
Dec. 1996. The HyperTextBooks. 5 May 2004 <http://papyr.com/
hypertextbooks/engl_126/ads.htm>.

Ebonics. The LINGUIST List. 26 Apr. 2004 <http://linguistlist.org/top-
ics/ebonics/>.

Ebonics Information Page. 25 Oct. 2001. Center for Applied Linguistics. 26 Apr. 2004 <http://www.cal.org/ebonics/>.

Johnson, Ellen. *Comments on Ebonics.* 27 Oct. 1998. Berry College. 26
Apr. 2004 <http://fsweb.berry.edu/academic/hass/ejohnson/
ebonics.htm>.

LSA Resolution on the Oakland "Ebonics" Issue. 3 Jan. 1997. Linguistics Society of America (LSA). 26 Apr 2004 <http://www.lsadc.org/
resolutions/index.php?aaa=ebonics.htm>.

Novak, Stanley M. *American Shibboleth: Ebonics.* Sep. 2000. Cambridge Scientific Abstracts. 26 Apr. 2004 <http://www.csa.com/
hottopics/ebonics/overview.html>.

Original Oakland Resolution on Ebonics. The LINGUIST List/The City
of Oakland School Board. 26 Apr. 2004 <http://linguistlist.org/top-
ics/ebonics/ebonics-res1.html>.

*Position Statement of the TESOL Board on African American Vernacular
English.* March 1997. Teachers of English to Speakers of Other

Languages (TESOL). 3 May 2004 <http://www.tesol.org/assoc/statements/africanamericanenglish.html>.

The Real Ebonics Debate: Power, Language, and the Education of African-American Children. Rethinking Schools Online 12.1 (1997). 26 Apr. 2004 <http://www.rethinkingschools.org/archive/12_01/12_01.shtml>.

Resolution on the Application of Dialect Knowledge to Education. 11 Mar. 1997. American Association for Applied Linguistics. 5 May 2004 <http://www.aaal.org/pages/resolutions.html#Dialect>.

Schiffman, Harold. *Bibliographies on the Subject of African-American Vernacular English (AAVE) and/or Black English.* 22 Mar. 2001. University of Pennsylvania. 26 Apr. 2004 <http://ccat.sas.upenn.edu/~haroldfs/540/handouts/aave/aave.html>.

Sidnell, Jack. *African American Vernacular English (Ebonics).* University of New England (Australia). 26 Apr. 2004 <http://www.une.edu.au/langnet/aave.htm>.

Statement on Ebonics. Conference on College Composition and Communication. 5 May 2004 <http://www.ncte.org/about/over/positions/level/coll/107644.htm>.

Wilce, Jim. A collection of articles and editorials on AAVE/BEV published in newspapers. Northern Arizona University. 26 Apr. 2004 <http://jan.ucc.nau.edu/~jmw22/aaveeditorials.html>.

Glossary

African American English (AAE): the nonstandard variety of English spoken by many African Americans; also known as **Black English, Ebonics,** or **African American Vernacular English (AAVE)**

African American rhetoric: the set of discourse strategies that represent how many African Americans use language

African American Vernacular English: common everyday English spoken by many African Americans

Afrocentric view of AAE: the theory that AAE is more African than English in origin

alternative rhetorics: discourse that does not follow the conventions of Western rhetoric

aspect: whether an action is completed or recurring

audiolingual pattern practice: listening and speaking exercises that require repetition and rote learning

bidialectalists: people who believe that speakers and writers should switch from nonstandard to Standard English to suit the occasion

Black English: a term often used instead of **African American English,** even though theoretically it could encompass the languages of *all* English-speaking Blacks

Black Standard English: a language that combines **Standard Written English** grammar with the rhetorical style that marks authors and speakers as black

broken English: a fractured form of speech without logic or rules

call-response: "spontaneous verbal and non-verbal interaction between speaker and listener in which all of the speaker's statements ('calls') are punctuated by expressions ('responses') from the listener" (Smitherman, *Talkin and Testifyin* 104)

camouflaged forms: constructions that look like those in other varieties of a language but possess unique uses or meanings in a particular dialect

code-switching: switching from one dialect to another to suit the occasion

cognitive deficit theories: theories that hold that nonstandard speech is a sign of limited intelligence

comment: all of the information pertinent to the **topic** of a sentence

competence: everything a person knows about language, e.g., rules for grammar, pronunciation, and meaning; vocabulary; reading and writing skills; language learning strategies

contrastive analysis: the juxtaposition of features of two languages

contrastive rhetoric: a rhetoric that views all languages as cultural phenomena, each with its unique linguistic and rhetorical conventions

creole: a fully developed language that evolves when a **pidgin** is taught to the next generation

Creolist view of AAE: the theory that AAE evolved from a **pidgin** that fused English and West African languages

current traditional rhetoric: a product-oriented approach that focuses on mastering rules of grammar and composition

deep structure: the underlying meaning of a sentence

dialects: variations of a language that are mutually intelligible but include some grammatical and/or pronunciation patterns that are unique to speakers in certain regions, social classes, or ethnic groups

dialect interference: a process by which a person's first dialect could lead to certain types of errors in a second dialect

diphthong: a complex vowel sound created by gliding from one vowel to another, as in *ou* in the word *house*

directness: a verbally aggressive way of speaking or writing

Dozens: a verbal game in which one insults the listener's relative (typically "yo mama") instead of the listener

Ebonics: languages spoken by people of African descent in the Caribbean and United States

eradicationists: people who wish to eliminate the use of nonstandard English

error analysis: the process of identifying the pattern and source of errors

Eurocentric view of AAE: the theory that AAE is a variety of English sharing more features with British and American English dialects than with West African languages

field dependence: the tendency to see "the big picture," to see the relationship of people and things to the whole

High Talk: ornate diction and exceedingly formal syntax

hypercorrections: incorrect forms or structures that stem from overgeneralizing rules

immersion: the use of and exposure to only the target language

interdialect: the personal dialect that results from simplifying forms and overgeneralizing rules in order to learn a new language

language: a system of (1) pronunciation rules (**phonology**), (2) rules that convey meaning (**semantics**), and (3) grammatical rules (**syntax**)

language interference: the tendency for a person's first language to influence the errors the person produces while learning a second language

linking verb: a verb that links the subject to a word that describes or renames the subject

metalinguistic awareness: a consciousness of the features and functions of language

miscue: an accidental miscommunication, as when a person inadvertently reads words or letters that are not on the page

model: to perform a target behavior (instead of correcting the undesired form) so that the observer can emulate it

narrative sequencing: storytelling

performance: what and how a person communicates at any given time in the form required

phonology: language rules governing pronunciation

pidgin: a simplified language that is created for limited and targeted communication between two communities that speak different languages

pluralists: people who accept nonstandard and standard English as linguistic equals in all walks of life

semantic inversion: giving traditionally negative words positive connotations

semantics: language rules that convey meaning

signifyin: "the verbal art of insult in which a speaker humorously puts down, talks about, needles . . . the listener. . . . [C]ulturally approved method of talking about somebody—usually through verbal indirection" (Smitherman, *Talkin and Testifyin*, 118–19)

slang: short-lived, informal words coined and shared by a limited group, typically musicians, hustlers, or teenagers of a particular region or social class

speech community: a group of people who share a dialect or language

Standard American English: the variety of English privileged in U.S. academic, government, and professional circles as well as the mainstream media; varies somewhat according to region; also known as **Standard English**

Standard English: the variety of English that is privileged in a society (see **Standard American English**)

Standard Written English (SWE): the U.S. standard for academic and professional writing

stereotype threat: "the threat of being viewed through the lens of a negative stereotype, or the fear of doing something that would inadvertently confirm that stereotype" (Steele)

syntax: grammatical rules

tense: the time of an action

testify: to tell the truth about God's goodness

toast: a tribute to a hustler or some other notorious character who repeatedly outsmarts the enemy

tonal semantics: the use of rhythm and inflection to express meaning, especially in African **tone languages**

tone languages: languages in which tone conveys meaning

topic: all of the information preceding the verb in a sentence

vernacular: common everyday language

voiced: uttered with vibrating vocal chords, producing sounds like the *b* in *big*

voiceless: uttered without a vibration of the vocal chords, producing sounds like the *p* in *pig*

WORKS CITED

Adger, Carolyn Temple. "Dialect Education: Not Only for Oakland." *ERIC/CLL News Bulletin* 20.2 (March 1997). 24 Jan. 2002 <www.cal.org/resources/News/199703/9703Dialect.html>.

Alim, H. Samy. "'We Are the Streets': African American Language and the Strategic Construction of a Street Conscious Identity." *Black Linguistics: Language, Society, and Politics in Africa and the Americas*. Ed. Sinfree Makoni, Geneva Smitherman, Arnetha Ball, and Arthur Spears. London: Routledge, 2003. 40–59.

Alvarez, Louis, and Andrew Kolker, prods. *American Tongues*. Videocassette. New York: Center for New American Media, 1987.

American Association for Applied Linguistics. "Resolution on the Application of Dialect Knowledge to Education." 1997. 21 July 2003 <www.aaal.org/pages/resolutions.html>.

Angle, Burr. "Freshman English Applications of Current Research in Black English." *Linguistic Perspectives on Black English*. Ed. Philip Luelsdorff. Regensburg: H. Carl, 1975. 143–54.

Anokye, Akua Duku, and Jaqueline Brice-Finch. *Get It Together: Readings about African American Life*. New York: Longman, 2003.

Arkhurst, Joyce Cooper. "Why Spider Lives in Ceilings." *The Adventures of Spider: West African Folktales*. 1964. Boston: Little, Brown, 1992.

Arthur, Bradford. "Teaching English to Minority Groups." *Teaching English as a Second or Foreign Language*. Ed. Marianne Celce-Murcia and Lois McIntosh. Rowley, MA: Newbury House, 1979. 270–76.

Asante, Molefi Kete. *The Afrocentric Idea*. Philadelphia: Temple UP, 1987.

Bailey, Guy, and Erik Thomas. "Some Aspects of African-American Vernacular English Phonology." *African American English*. Ed.

Salikoko S. Mufwene, John Rickford, Guy Bailey, and John Baugh. London: Routledge, 1998. 85–109.

Baldwin, James. "If Black English Isn't a Language, Then Tell Me, What Is?" *New York Times* 27 July 1979. 16 Aug. 2002 <http://partners.nytimes.com/books/98/03/29/specials/baldwin-english.html>.

Balester, Valerie M. *Cultural Divide: A Study of African-American College-Level Writers.* Portsmouth, NH: Boynton/Cook, 1993.

Ball, Arnetha F. "Community-Based Learning in Urban Settings as a Model for Educational Reform." *Applied Behavioral Science Review* 3 (1998): 127–46.

———. "Cultural Preference and the Expository Writing of African-American Adolescents." *Written Communication* 9 (1992): 501-32.

———. "Evaluating the Writing of Culturally and Linguistically Diverse Students: The Case of the African American Vernacular English Speaker." *Evaluating Writing: The Role of Teachers' Knowledge about Text, Learning, and Culture.* Ed. Charles R. Cooper and Lee Odell. Urbana, IL: National Council of Teachers of English, 1999. 225–48.

———. "Language, Learning, and Linguistic Competence of African American Children: Torrey Revisited." *Linguistics and Education* 7 (1995): 23–46.

———. "Playin' the Dozens: Bringing Literacies to Life in Composition Classrooms." Paper. Conf. on Coll. Composition and Communication Convention. New York Hilton, New York. March 2003.

———. "Text Design Patterns in the Writing of Urban African American Students: Teaching to the Cultural Strengths of Students in Multicultural Settings." *Urban Education* 30 (1995): 253–89.

Ball, Arnetha, and Ted Lardner. "Dispositions toward Language: Teacher Constructs of Knowledge and the Ann Arbor Black English Case." *College Composition and Communication* 48 (1997): 469–85.

Bartholomae, David. "The Study of Error." *College Composition and Communication* 31 (1980): 253–69.

Baugh, John. *Beyond Ebonics: Linguistic Pride and Racial Prejudice.* New York: Oxford UP, 2000.

———. *Out of the Mouths of Slaves: African American Language and Educational Malpractice*. Austin: U of Texas P, 1999.

Beason, Larry. "Ethos and Error: How Business People React to Errors." *College Composition and Communication* 53 (2001): 33–64.

Blackshire-Belay, Aisha. "Linguistic Dimension of Global Africa: Ebonics as International Languages of African Peoples." *Ebonics and Language Education of African Ancestry Students*. Ed. Clinton Crawford. New York: Sankofa, 2001. 164–90.

Botan, Carl, and Geneva Smitherman. "Black English in the Integrated Workplace." *Journal of Black Studies* 22 (1991): 168–85.

Boykin, A. Wade. "Afrocultural Expression and Its Implications for Schooling." *Teaching Diverse Populations: Formulating a Knowledge Base*. Ed. Etta R. Hollins, Joyce E. King, and Warren C. Hayman. Albany: SUNY P, 1994. 243–73.

Brown, Claude. *Manchild in the Promised Land*. New York: Signet, 1965.

Brown, H. Rap [Jamil Al-Amin]. *Die, Nigger, Die!* New York: Dial, 1969.

Brown, H. Douglas. *Principles of Language Learning and Teaching*. 2nd ed. Englewood Cliffs, NJ: Prentice Hall, 1987.

Brown, Roscoe C. Jr. "Testing Black Student Writers." *Writing Assessment: Issues and Strategies*. Ed. Karen L. Greenberg, Harvey S. Wiener, and Richard A. Donovan. New York: Longman, 1986. 98–108.

Campbell, Jay R., Clyde M. Reese, Christine O'Sullivan, and J. A. Dossey. *NAEP 1994 Trends in Academic Progress*. Washington, DC: National Center for Education Statistics, 1996.

Campbell, Kermit E. "Real Niggaz's Don't Die: African American Students Speaking Themselves into Their Writing." *Writing in Multicultural Settings*. Ed. Carol Severino, Juan C. Guerra, and Johnnella E. Butler. New York: Modern Language Association, 1997. 67–78.

———. "The *Signifying Monkey* Revisited: Vernacular Discourse and African American Personal Narratives." *Journal of Advanced Composition* 14 (1994). 14 August 2003 <http://jac.gsu.edu/jac/14.2/Articles/8.htm>.

Canagarajah, A. Suresh. "Safe Houses in the Contact Zone: Coping Strategies of African-American Students in the Academy." *College Composition and Communication* 48 (1997):173–96.

Chapelle, Carol, and Cheryl Roberts. "Ambiguity Tolerance and Field Independence as Predictors of Proficiency in English as a Second Language." *Language Learning* 36 (1986): 27–45.

Chaplin, Miriam. "A Closer Look at Black and White Students' Assessment Essays." *Iowa English Bulletin* 38 (1990): 15–27.

Coleman, Charles F. "Our Students Write with Accents." *College Composition and Communication* 48 (1997): 486–500.

Coleman, James. *Progress, Proficiency and Motivation among British University Language Learners*. CLCS Occasional Paper No. 40. Dublin: Trinity College, Centre for Language and Communication Studies, 1995. ERIC Doc. ED383221.

Conference on College Composition and Communication (CCCC). *Students' Right to Their Own Language*. Spec. issue of *College Composition and Communication* 25 (1974).

Connor, Ulla. "Contrastive Rhetoric: Implications for Teachers of Writing in Multicultural Classrooms." *Writing in Multicultural Settings*. Ed. Carol Severino, Juan C. Guerra, Johnnella E. Butler. New York: Modern Language Association, 1997. 198–208.

Connors, Robert J. "Mechanical Correctness as a Focus in Composition Instruction." *College Composition and Communication* 36 (1985): 61–72.

Crawford, Clinton, ed. *Ebonics and Language Education of African Ancestry Students*. New York: Sankofa, 2001.

Cromwell, Otelia, Lorenzo Dow Turner, and Eva B. Dykes. *Readings from Negro Authors, for Schools and Colleges*. New York: Harcourt, Brace, 1931.

Crystal, David. *A Dictionary of Linguistics and Phonetics*. 4th ed. Oxford: Blackwell, 1997.

Cukor-Avila, Patricia, and Guy Bailey. "The Spread of Urban AAVE: A Case Study." *Sociolinguistic Variation: Data, Theory, and Analysis: Selected Papers from NWAV 23 at Stanford*. Stanford: Center for the Study of Language and Information, Stanford University, 1996. 469–85.

Dandy, Evelyn Baker. *Black Communications: Breaking Down the Barriers*. Chicago: African American Images, 1991.

Debose, Charles, and Nicholas Faraclas. "An Africanist Approach to the Linguistic Study of Black English: Getting to the Roots of Tense-Aspect-Modality and Copula Systems in Afro-American." *Africanisms in Afro-American Language Varieties*. Ed. Salikoko S. Mufwene. Athens: U of Georgia P, 1993. 364–87.

Delpit, Lisa. "The Silenced Dialogue." *Other People's Children: Cultural Conflict in the Classsroom*. New York: New Press, 1995. 21–47.

———. "What Should Teachers Do? Ebonics and Culturally Responsive Instruction." *The Real Ebonics Debate: Power, Language, and the Education of African-American Children*. Ed. Theresa Perry and Lisa Delpit. Boston: Beacon, 1998. 17–26.

Deutsch, Martin, Irwin Katz, and Arthur R. Jensen, eds. *Social Class, Race, and Psychological Development*. New York: Holt, Rinehart, and Winston, 1968.

Dillard, J. L., *Black English: Its History and Usage in the United States*. New York: Random House, 1972.

Douglass, Frederick. *Narrative of the Life of Frederick Douglass, an American Slave*. New York: Signet, 1968.

Dunbar, Paul Laurence. "The Poet." *Afro-American Writing: An Anthology of Prose and Poetry*. Vol. I. Ed. Richard A. Long and Eugenia W. Collier. New York: New York UP, 1972. 220.

Edwards, Walter F., and Donald Winford, eds. *Verb Phrase Patterns in Black English and Creole*. Detroit: Wayne State UP, 1991.

Elbow, Peter. "Vernacular Englishes in the Writing Classroom: Probing the Culture of Literacy." *ALT DIS: Alternative Discourses and the Academy*. Ed. Christopher Schroeder, Helen Fox, and Patricia Bizzell. Portsmouth, NH: Boynton/Cook, Heinemann, 2002. 126–38.

Ellis, Rod. *The Study of Second Language Acquisition*. Oxford: Oxford UP, 1994.

Equiano, Olaudah. "The Interesting Narrative of the Life of Olaudah Equiano, or Gustavus Vassa, the African." *The Classic Slave Narratives*. Ed. Henry Louis Gates Jr. New York: Penguin, 1987.

Evans, Henry L. "An Afrocentric Multicultural Writing Project." *Writing in Multicultural Settings.* Ed. Carol Severino, Juan C. Guerra, and Johnnella E. Butler. New York: Modern Language Association, 1997. 273–86.

Fanon, Frantz. *Black Skin, White Masks.* Trans. Charles Lam Markmann. New York: Grove, 1967.

Farr, Marcia, and Harvey Daniels. *Language Diversity and Writing Instruction.* Urbana, IL: ERIC Clearinghouse on Reading and Communication Skills, 1986.

Farr, Marcia, and Gloria Nardini. "Essayist Literacy and Sociolinguistic Difference." *Assessment of Writing: Politics, Policies, and Practices.* Ed. Edward M. White, William D. Lutz, and Sandra Kamusikiri. New York: Modern Language Association, 1996. 108–19.

Farrell, Thomas J. "IQ and Standard English." *College Composition and Communication* 34 (1983): 470–84.

Fasold, Ralph W. "What Can an English Teacher Do about Nonstandard Dialect?" *English Record* 21 (1971): 82–91.

Feigenbaum, Irwin. "The Use of Nonstandard English in Teaching Standard: Contrast and Comparison." *Teaching Standard English in the Inner City.* Ed. Ralph W. Fasold and Roger W. Shuy. Washington, DC: Center for Applied Linguistics, 1970. 87–104.

Flower, Linda, and John Hayes. "The Dynamics of Composing: Making Plans and Juggling Constraints." *Cognitive Processes in Writing.* Ed. Lee W. Gregg and Erwin R. Steinberg. Hillsdale, NJ: Lawrence Erlbaum, 1980. 31–50.

Fordham, Signithia, and John Ogbu U. "Black Students' School Success: Coping with the 'Burden of Acting White.'" *Urban Review* 18 (1986): 176–206.

Foster, Michele. "Effective Black Teachers: A Literature Review." *Teaching Diverse Populations: Formulating a Knowledge Base.* Ed. Etta R. Hollins, Joyce E. King, and Warren C. Hayman. Albany: SUNY P, 1994. 225–41.

Fox, Thomas. "Repositioning the Profession: Teaching Writing to African American Students." *Journal of Advanced Composition* 12 (1992): 291–301.

Freire, Paulo. *Pedagogy of the Oppressed.* 1970. New York: Continuum, 1990.

Gardner, Robert C., and Wallace E. Lambert. *Attitudes and Motivation in Second-Language Learning.* Rowley, MA: Newbury House, 1972.

Gee, James Paul. *Literacy, Discourse, and Linguistics: Essays by James Paul Gee.* Spec. issue of *Journal of Education* 171 (1989).

Gilmore, Perry. "Spelling 'Mississippi': Recontextualizing a Literacy-Related Speech Event. *Anthropology and Education Quarterly* 14 (1983): 235–55.

Gilyard, Keith. "African American Contributions to Composition Studies." *College Composition and Communication* 50 (1999): 626–44.

———. "It Ain't Hard to Tell: Distinguishing Fact from Fallacy in the Ebonics Controversy." *Ebonics and Language Education of African Ancestry Students.* Ed. Clinton Crawford. New York: Sankofa, 2001. 202–13.

———. *Let's Flip the Script: An African American Discourse on Language, Literature, and Learning.* Detroit: Wayne State UP, 1996.

Gilyard, Keith, and Elaine Richardson. "Students' Right to Possibility: Basic Writing and African American Rhetoric." *Insurrections: Approaches to Resistance in Composition Studies.* Ed. Andrea Greenbaum. Albany: SUNY P, 2001. 37–51.

Green, Lisa J. *African American English: A Linguistic Introduction.* Cambridge: Cambridge UP, 2002.

Hairston, Maxine. "Not All Errors Are Created Equal: Nonacademic Readers in the Professions Respond to Lapses in Usage." *College English* 43 (1981): 794–806.

Hamp-Lyons, Liz. "Exploring Bias in Essay Tests." *Writing in Multicultural Settings.* Ed. Carol Severino, Juan C. Guerra, Johnnella E. Butler. New York: Modern Language Association, 1997. 51–66.

Hansen, Jacqueline, and Charles Stansfield. "The Relationship of Field-Dependent-Independent Cognitive Styles to Foreign Language Achievement." *Language Learning* 31 (1981): 349–67.

Harris-Wright, Kelli. "Enhancing Bidialectalism in Urban African American Students." *Making the Connection: Language and Academic Achievement among African American Students.* Ed. Carolyn Temple Adger, Donna Christian, and Orlando L. Taylor. Washington, DC: Center for Applied Linguistics, 1999. 53–60.

Hartwell, Patrick. "Dialect Interference in Writing: A Critical View." *Research in the Teaching of English* 14 (1980): 101–18.

Hatch, Evelyn. *Discourse and Language Education.* Cambridge: Cambridge UP, 1992.

Hawhee, Debra. "Composition History and the *Harbrace College Handbook.*" *College Composition and Communication* 50 (1999): 504–23.

Heilker, Paul. "Official Feasts and Carnivals: Student Writing and Public Ritual." *Teaching English in the Two-Year College* 29 (2001): 77–84.

Herrnstein, Richard J., and Charles Murray. *The Bell Curve: Intelligence and Class Structure in American Life.* New York: Free Press, 1994.

Hilliard, Asa G. III, Lucretia Payton-Stewart, and Larry Obadele Williams, eds. *Infusion of African and African American Content in the School Curriculum: Proceedings of the First National Conference, October 1989.* Morristown, NJ: Aaron, 1990.

Hillocks, George Jr. *Research on Written Composition: New Directions for Teaching.* Urbana, IL: National Council of Teachers of English, 1986.

Holm, John. "Variability of the Copula in Black English and Its Creole Kin." *American Speech* 59 (1984): 291–309.

Holmes, David. "Fighting Back by *Writing* Black: Beyond Racially Reductive Composition Theory." *Race, Rhetoric, and Composition.* Ed. Keith Gilyard. Portsmouth, NH: Boynton/Cook, 1999. 53–66.

Hoover, Mary. "A Culturally Appropriate Approach to Teaching Basic (and Other) Critical Communication Skills to Black College Students." *Negro Educational Review* 33 (1982): 14–27.

———. "The Nairobi Day School: An African American Independent School, 1966–1984." *Journal of Negro Education* 61 (1992): 201–10.

Hoover, Mary, and Robert L. Politzer. "Bias in Composition Tests with Suggestions for a Culturally Appropriate Assessment Technique." *Variation in Writing: Functional and Linguistic-Cultural Differences.* Ed. Marcia Farr Whiteman. Hillsdale, NJ: Lawrence Erlbaum, 1981.

Hopper, Paul J., and Elizabeth Closs Traugott. *Grammaticalization.* Cambridge: Cambridge UP, 1993.

Howard, Rebecca Moore. "The Great Wall of African American Vernacular English in the American College Classroom." *Journal of Advanced Composition* 16 (1996): 265–83.

Hudson, Richard. "Grammar Teaching and Writing Skills: The Research Evidence." *Syntax in the Schools: The Journal of the Assembly for the Teaching of English Grammar* 17.1 (2000): 1–6.

Hurston, Zora Neale. *Dust Tracks on a Road*. 1942. New York: HarperPerennial, 1991.

Jackson, Ronald L. II, and Elaine B. Richardson, eds. *Understanding African American Rhetoric: Classical Origins to Contemporary Innovations*. New York: Routledge, 2003.

Jensen, Arthur R. "How Much Can We Boost IQ and Scholastic Achievement?" *Harvard Educational Review* 39 (1969): 1–123.

Jones-Jackson, Patricia. *When Roots Die: Endangered Traditions on the Sea Islands*. Athens: U of Georgia P, 1989.

Kamusikiri, Sandra. "African American English and Writing Assessment: An Afrocentric Approach." *Assessment of Writing: Politics, Policies, Practices*. Ed. Edward M. White, William D. Lutz, and Sandra Kamusikiri. New York: Modern Language Association, 1996. 187–203.

Krashen, Stephen D. *Principles and Practice in Second Language Acquisition*. New York: Pergamon, 1982.

Kroch, Anthony, and William Labov. "Resolution in Response to Arthur Jensen (1969)." *Linguistic Society of America Bulletin*. Washington, DC: Linguistic Society of America, March 1972.

Kutz, Eleanor. "Between Students' Language and Academic Discourse: Interlanguage as Middle Ground." *College English* 48 (1986): 385–96.

Labov, William. "Academic Ignorance and Black Intelligence." *Atlantic Monthly* June 1972. 3 June 2003 <www.theatlantic.com>.

———. "Can Reading Failure Be Reversed?: A Linguistic Approach to the Question." *Literacy among African-American Youth: Issues in Learning, Teaching, and Schooling*. Ed. Vivian L. Gadsden and Daniel A. Wagner. Cresskill, NJ: Hampton, 1995. 39–68.

———. *Language in the Inner City: Studies in the Black English Vernacular*. Philadelphia: U of Pennsylvania P, 1972.

———. "Testimony Before the U.S. Senate: Senate Appropriation Committee's Subcommittee on Labor, Health, and Human Services, and Education, chaired by Senator Arlen Specter." 23 January 1997. *Beyond Ebonics: Linguistic Pride and Racial Prejudice.* John Baugh. New York: Oxford UP, 2000.

Ladson-Billings, Gloria. "Who Will Teach Our Children? Preparing Teachers to Successfully Teach African American Students." *Teaching Diverse Populations: Formulating a Knowledge Base.* Ed. Etta R. Hollins, Joyce E. King, and Warren C. Hayman. Albany: SUNY P, 1994. 129–42.

Language Curriculum Research Group. "Letter to the Editor." *Crisis* 78 (1971): 174.

Lee, Carol D. *Signifying as a Scaffold for Literary Interpretation: The Pedagogical Implications of an African American Discourse Genre.* Urbana, IL: National Council of Teachers of English, 1993.

Lee, Margaret Giles, Joyce M. Jarrett, Doreatha Drummond Mbalia, eds. *Heritage: African American Readings for Writing.* 2nd ed. Upper Saddle River, NJ: Prentice Hall, 2002.

LeMoine, Noma. *English for Your Success: A Language Development Program for African American Children.* Maywood, NJ: Peoples Publishing Group, 1999.

Leonard, Donald J., and Jeanette W. Gilsdorf. "Language in Change: Academics' and Executives' Perceptions of Usage Errors." *Journal of Business Communication* 27 (1990): 137–58.

Lewis, Laurie, and Elizabeth Farris. *Remedial Education at Higher Education Institutions in Fall 1995.* Washington, DC: U.S. Department of Education, National Center for Educational Statistics, 1996.

Lewis, Shirley A. "Practical Aspects of Teaching Composition to Bidialectal Students: The Nairobi Method." *Variation in Writing: Functional and Linguistic-Cultural Difference.* Ed. Marcia Farr Whiteman. Hillsdale, NJ: Lawrence Erlbaum, 1981. 189–96.

Linguistic Society of America. *LSA Resolution on the Oakland "Ebonics" Issue.* 3 Jan. 1997. 26 April 2004 <www.lsadc.org/resolutions/index.php?aaa=ebonics.htm>.

Lukmani, Yasmeen M. "Motivation to Learn and Language Proficiency." *Language Learning* 22 (1972): 261–73.

Macnamara, John. "Comparison between First and Second Language Learning." *Working Papers on Bilingualism* 7 (1975): 71–94.

Maddahian, Ebrahim, and Ambition Padi Sandamela. *Academic English Mastery Program: 1998–99 Evaluation Report.* Los Angeles: Los Angeles Unified School District, 2000. ERIC Doc. ED440538.

Mahiri, Jabari. *Shooting for Excellence: African American and Youth Culture in New Century Schools.* Urbana, IL, and New York: National Council of Teachers of English and Teachers College Press, 1998.

Major, Clarence, ed. *Juba to Jive: A Dictionary of African-American Slang.* New York: Penguin, 1994.

Malcolm X. "Message to the Grassroots." *Malcolm X Speaks: Selected Speeches and Statements.* 1965. New York: Grove Weidenfeld, 1990.

Malcolm X, with Alex Hailey. *The Autobiography of Malcolm X.* New York: Ballantine, 1965.

Martin, Stefan, and Walt Wolfram. "The Sentence in African-American Vernacular English." *African-American English: Structure, History, and Use.* Ed. Salikoko S. Mufwene, John Rickford, Guy Bailey, and John Baugh. London: Routledge, 1998. 11–36.

McNenny, Gerri, and Sallyanne H. Fitzgerald, eds. *Mainstreaming Basic Writers: Politics and Pedagogies of Access.* Mahwah, NJ: Lawrence Erlbaum, 2001.

McWhorter, John. *Spreading the Word: Language and Dialect in America.* Portsmouth, NH: Heinemann, 2000.

———. *The Word on the Street: Fact and Fable about American English.* New York: Plenum, 1998.

Meier, Terry. "'Listen to Your Students': An Interview with Oakland High School English Teacher Hafeezah AdamaDavia Dalji: Teaching Teachers about Black Communications." *The Real Ebonics Debate: Power, Language, and the Education of African-American Children.* Ed. Theresa Perry and Lisa Delpit. Boston: Beacon, 1998. 105–15.

Mix, Julie Ann. "Evidencing Nonstandard Feature Dynamics: 'Speak Aloud and Write' Protocols by African American Freshman Composition Students." *Written Communication* 20 (2003): 307–32.

Moore, Renee (1998, Summer). "Teaching Standard English to African American Students: Conceptualizing the Research Project." *Breadloaf Rural Teacher Network.* 12–15. [Newsletter, Middlebury College]

Morgan, Marcyliena. "More Than a Mood or an Attitude: Discourse and Verbal Genres in African-American Culture." *African-American English: Structure, History, and Use*. Ed. Salikoko S. Mufwene, John Rickford, Guy Bailey, and John Baugh. London: Routledge, 1998. 251–81.

———. "Nuthin' but a G Thang'": Grammar and Language Ideology in Hip Hop Identity." *Sociocultural and Historical Contexts of African American English*. Ed. Sonja L. Lanehart. Amsterdam: John Benjamins, 2001. 187–209.

Morrow, Daniel H. "Dialect Interference in Writing: Another Critical View." *Research in the Teaching of English* 19 (1985): 154–80.

Mountford, Roxanne. "Let Them Experiment: Accommodating Diverse Discourse Practices in Large-Scale Writing Assessment." *Assessment of Writing: Politics, Policies, Practices*. Ed. Edward M. White, William D. Lutz, and Sandra Kamusikiri. New York: Modern Language Association, 1996. 366–96.

Mufwene, Salikoko S. "What Is African American English?" *Sociocultural and Historical Contexts of African American English*. Ed. Sonja L. Lanehart. Amsterdam: John Benjamins, 2001. 21–51.

Nehusi, Kimani S. K. "From Medew Netjer to Ebonics." *Ebonics and Language Education of African Ancestry Students*. Ed. Clinton Crawford. New York: Sankofa, 2001. 56–122.

Noguchi, Rei R. *Grammar and the Teaching of Writing: Limits and Possibilities*. Urbana, IL: National Council of Teachers of English, 1991.

Noonan-Wagner, Desley. *Black Writers in the Classroom: A Question of Language Experience, not Grammar*. Paper. Conf. on Coll. Composition and Communication Convention. Washington Hilton, Washington, DC. March 1980. ERIC Doc. ED189599.

Oller, John W., A. Hudson, and Phyllis Liu. "Attitudes and Attained Proficiency in ESL: A Sociolinguistic Study of Native Speakers of Chinese in the United States." *Language Learning* 27 (1977): 1–27.

Oller, John W. Jr., and Seid M. Ziahosseiny. "The Contrastive Analysis Hypothesis and Spelling Errors. *Language Learning* 20 (1970): 183–89.

O'Neal, Verley, and Tom Trabasso. "Is There a Correspondence between Sound and Spelling? Some Implications for Black English Speakers." *Black English: A Seminar*. Ed. Deborah Sears Harrison and Tom Trabasso. Hillsdale, NJ: Lawrence Erlbaum, 1976. 171–90.

Palacas, Arthur L. "Liberating American Ebonics from Euro-English." *College English* 63 (2001): 326–52.

Parker, Henry H., and Marilyn I. Crist. *Teaching Minorities to Play the Corporate Language Game.* Columbia: University of South Carolina, National Resource Center for the Freshman Year Experience, 1995.

Perl, Sondra, and Nancy Wilson. *Through Teachers' Eyes: Portraits of Writing Teachers at Work.* Portsmouth, NH: Heinemann, 1986.

Persky, Hilary R., Mary C. Daane, and Ying Jin. *The Nation's Report Card: Writing 2002.* July 2003. National Assessment of Educational Progress. 25 July 2003. http://nces.ed.gov/nationsreportcard/pubs/main2002/2003529.asp.

Piestrup, Ann McCormick. *Black Dialect Interference and Accommodation of Reading Instruction in First Grade.* Monograph of the Language-Behavior Research Laboratory, No. 4. Berkeley: University of California, 1973.

Pitts, Walter F. *Old Ship of Zion: The Afro-Baptist Ritual in the African Diaspora.* New York: Oxford UP, 1993.

Pollard, Diane, and Cheryl Ajirotutu. "School Restructuring in an African-Centered Educational Model. *Illinois School Journal* 75 (1997): 41–54.

Poplack, Shana, ed. *The English History of African American English.* Oxford: Blackwell, 2000.

Raspberry, William. "To Throw in a Lot of 'Bes,' or Not? A Conversation on Ebonics." *Washington Post* 26 Dec. 1996: A27.

Ratteray, Joan Davis. *Center Shift: An African-Centered Approach for the Multicultural Curriculum.* Washington, DC: Institute for Independent Education, 1990. ERIC Doc. ED320983.

Redd, Teresa M. "An Afrocentric Curriculum in a Composition Classroom: Motivating Students to Read, Write, and Think." Paper. Conf. on Coll. Composition and Communication Convention. Sheraton Harbor Island Hotel, San Diego, CA, 1993. ERIC Doc. ED362898.

———. "'How I Got Ovah': Success Stories of African American Composition Students, Part II." Paper. Con. on Coll. Composition and Communication Convention. Adam's Mark Hotel, Denver, CO, 2001. ERIC Doc. ED455537.

———, ed. *Revelations: An Anthology of Expository Essays by and about Blacks.* 4th ed. Boston: Pearson, 2002.

———. "'Tryin to Make a Dolla Outa Fifteen Cent': Teaching Composition with the Internet at an HBCU." *Computers and Composition* 20 (2003): 359–73.

———. "Untapped Resources: 'Styling' in Black Students' Writing for Black Audiences." *Composing Social Identity in Written Language.* Ed. Donald L. Rubin. Hillsdale, NJ: Lawrence Erlbaum, 1995. 221–40.

Reed, Carol E. "Adapting TESL Approaches to the Teaching of Written Standard English as a Second Dialect to Speakers of American Black English Vernacular." *TESOL Quarterly* 7 (1973): 289–307.

Richardson, Elaine. *African American Literacies.* London: Routledge, 2003.

———. "Critique on the Problematic of Implementing Afrocentricity into Traditional Curriculum: The Powers That Be." *Journal of Black Studies* 31 (2000): 196–213.

———. "Race, Class(es), Gender, and Age: The Making of Knowledge about Language Diversity." *Language Diversity in the Classroom: From Intention to Practice.* Ed. Geneva Smitherman and Victor Villaneuva. Carbondale: Southern Illinois UP, 2003. 40–66.

———. "'To Protect and Serve': African American Female Literacies." *College Composition and Communication* 53 (2002): 675–704.

Rickford, John R. *African American Vernacular English: Features, Evolution, Educational Implications.* Oxford: Blackwell, 1999.

———. "Ebonics and Education: Lessons from the Caribbean, Europe and the USA." *Ebonics and Language Education of African Ancestry Students.* Ed. Clinton Crawford. New York: Sankofa, 2001. 263–84.

———. "Language Diversity and Academic Achievement in the Education of African American Students: An Overview of the Issues." *Making the Connection: Language and Academic Achievement among African American Students.* Ed. Carolyn Temple Adger, Donna Christian, and Orlando L. Taylor. Washington, DC: Center for Applied Linguistics, 1999. 1–29.

Rickford, John Russell, and Russell John Rickford. *Spoken Soul: The Story of Black English.* New York: Wiley, 2000.

Science Research Associates (SRA). "Direct Instruction: Distar Language III." SRA Product Information. 14 June 2003 <www.sraonline.com/

index.php/home/curriculumsolutions/di/distarlanguage/distarlong copy/214>.

Shaughnessy, Mina P. *Errors and Expectations: A Guide for the Teacher of Basic Writing.* New York: Oxford UP, 1977.

Simpkins, Gary A., Grace Holt, and Charlesetta Simpkins. *Bridge: A Cross-Culture Reading Program.* Boston: Houghton Mifflin, 1977.

Simpkins, Gary A., and Charlesetta Simpkins. "Cross-Cultural Approach to Curriculum Development. *Black English and the Education of Black Children and Youth: Proceedings of the National Invitational Symposium on the King Decision.* Ed. Geneva Smitherman. Detroit: Center for Black Studies, Wayne State University, 1981. 221–40.

Smith, Ernie. "What Is Black English? What Is Ebonics?" *The Real Ebonics Debate: Power, Language, and the Education of African-American Children.* Ed. Theresa Perry and Lisa Delpit. Boston: Beacon, 1998. 49–58.

Smitherman, Geneva. *Black Talk: Words and Phrases from the Hood to the Amen Corner.* Rev. ed. Boston: Houghton Mifflin, 2000.

———. *Talkin and Testifyin: The Language of Black America.* 1977. Detroit: Wayne State UP, 1986.

———. *Talkin That Talk: Language, Culture, and Education in African America.* New York: Routledge, 2000.

———. "'What Go Round Come Round': *King* in Perspective." *Tapping Potential: English and Language Arts for the Black Learner.* Ed. Charlotte K. Brooks. Urbana, IL: National Council of Teachers of English, 1985. 41–62.

Spears, Arthur K. "African-American Language Use: Ideology and So-Called Obscenity." *African-American English: Structure, History, and Use.* Ed. Salikoko S. Mufwene, John Rickford, Guy Bailey, and John Baugh. London: Routledge, 1998. 226–50.

———. "The Black English Semi-Auxiliary 'Come.'" *Language* 58 (1982): 850–72.

———. "Directness in the Use of African American English." *Sociocultural and Historical Contexts of African American English.* Ed. Sonja L. Lanehart. Amsterdam and Philadelphia: John Benjamins, 2001. 239–59.

Steele, Claude M. "Thin Ice: 'Stereotype Threat' and Black College Students." *Atlantic* 284.2 (Aug. 1999): 44–47, 50–54. <http:www.the atlantic.com>.

Stewart, W. A. "Sociolinguistic Factors in the History of American Negro Dialects." 1967. *Black-White Speech Relationships.* Ed. Walt Wolfram and Nona H. Clarke. Washington, DC: Center for Applied Linguistics, 1971. 74–89.

Tauber, Robert T. *Self-Fulfilling Prophecy: A Practical Guide to Its Use in Education.* Westport, CT: Praeger, 1997.

Taylor, Hanni U. *Standard English, Black English, and Bidialectalism: A Controversy.* New York: P. Lang, 1989.

Taylor, Orlando L. "Testimony of Orlando L. Taylor on the Subject of 'Ebonics.'" *Making the Connection: Language and Academic Achievement among African American Students.* Ed. Carolyn Temple Adger, Donna Christian, and Orlando L. Taylor. Washington, DC: Center for Applied Linguistics, 1999. 169–75.

Teweles, B. "Motivation as a Two-Sided Coin: Motivational Differences between College-Level Chinese and Japanese Learners of EFL." *Texas Papers in Foreign Language Education* 2, 1995. ERIC Doc. ED416704.

Thiong'o, Ngugi wa. *Decolonising the Mind: The Politics of Language in African Literature.* Portsmouth, NH: Heinemann, 1994.

Thompson, Dorothy Perry. "Rescuing the Failed, Filed Away, and Forgotten: African Americans and Eurocentricity in Academic Argument." *Perspectives on Written Argument.* Ed. Deborah P. Berrill. Creskill, NJ: Hampton, 1996. 221–40.

Troutman, Denise. "African American Women: Talking That Talk." *Sociocultural and Historical Contexts of African American English.* Ed. Sonja L. Lanehart. Amsterdam: John Benjamins, 2001. 211–37.

———. "Whose Voice Is It Anyway? Marked Features in the Writing of Black English Speakers." *Writing in Multicultural Settings.* Ed. Carol Severino, Juan C. Guerra, Johnnella E. Butler. New York: Modern Language Association, 1997. 27–39.

Turner, Lorenzo Dow. *Africanisms in the Gullah Dialect.* 1949. Ann Arbor: U of Michigan P, 1973.

Van Keulen, Jean E., Gloria Toliver Weddington, and Charles E. DeBose. *Speech, Language, Learning, and the African American Child.* Boston: Allyn and Bacon, 1998.

Van Sertima, Ivan. "My Gullah Brother and I: Exploration into a Community's Language and Myth through Its Oral Tradition." *Black English: A Seminar.* Ed. Deborah Sears Harrison and Tom Trabasso. Hillsdale, NJ: Lawrence Erlbaum, 1976. 123–46.

Vaughn-Cooke, Anna F. "Lessons Learned from the Ebonics Controversy: Implications for Language Assessment." *Making the Connection: Language and Academic Achievement among African American Students.* Ed. Carolyn Temple Adger, Donna Christian, and Orlando L. Taylor. Washington, DC: Center for Applied Linguistics, 1999. 137–68.

Walker, Alice. *The Color Purple.* New York: Harcourt Brace Jovanovich, 1982.

Walker, Vanessa Siddle. "African American Teaching in the South, 1940–1960." *American Educational Research Journal* 38 (2001): 751–79.

Walvoord, Barbara E. Fassler. *Helping Students Write Well: A Guide for Teachers in All Disciplines.* 2nd ed. New York: Modern Language Association, 1986.

Wang, Xiao. Accommodating Marked Features of Ebonics in Freshman Essays: From a Narrative Essay to a Research Paper. Paper. Con. on Coll. Composition and Communication Convention. Minneapolis Hilton/Convention Center, MN, 2000. ERIC Doc. ED 442112.

Webb, Karen, and Sloan E. Williams. "Topic Shift Analysis: Organizational Strategies for Successful Writing." *CEA MidAtlantic Journal* 4 (1992): 50–57.

White, Edward M., and Leon L. Thomas. "Racial Minorities and Writing Skills Assessment in the California State University and Colleges." *College English* 43 (1981): 276–83.

Whiteman, Marcia Farr. "Dialect Influence in Writing." *Variation in Writing: Functional and Linguistic-Cultural Differences.* Ed. Marcia Farr Whiteman. Hillsdale, NJ: Lawrence Erlbaum, 1981. 153–66.

Whitten, Mary E., Winifred B. Horner, and Suzanne S. Webb. *Harbrace College Handbook.* 11th ed. New York: Harcourt Brace Jovanovich, 1990.

Williams, Robert L., ed. *Ebonics: The True Language of Black Folks.* St. Louis: Institute of Black Studies, 1975.

Wilson, Allison. "Black Dialect and the Freshman Writer." *Journal of Basic Writing* 4 (1985): 44–54.

Wolfram, Walter. "Repercussions from the Oakland Ebonics Controversy: The Critical Role of Dialect Awareness Programs." *Making the Connection: Language and Academic Achievement among African American Students.* Ed. Carolyn Temple Adger, Donna Christian, and Orlando L. Taylor. Washington, DC: Center for Applied Linguistics, 1999. 61–80.

Wolfram, Walter, Carolyn Temple Adger, and Donna Christian. *Dialects in Schools and Communities.* Mahwah, NJ: Lawrence Erlbaum, 1999.

Wolfram, Walter, and Natalie Schilling-Estes. *American English: Dialects and Variation.* Oxford: Blackwell, 1998.

Woodyard, Jeffrey Lynn. "Africological Theory and Criticism: Reconceptualizing Communication Constructs." *Understanding African American Rhetoric: Classical Origins to Contemporary Innovations.* Ed. Ronald L. Jackson II and Elaine B. Richardson. New York: Routledge, 2003. 133–54.

INDEX

AAE. *See* African American English
absent *be,* 9, 13
abstract thinking, 59
academic discourse, 50, 119
Academic English Mastery Program, 87, 100
"Academic Ignorance and Black Intelligence," 60
ace boon coon, 7
Adger, Carolyn Temple, 61, 64–65, 93
adjectives, 31
adverbs, 31
affective filter hypothesis, 68
African American English (AAE)
  as "broken" English, 4–7
  as dialect, 8–11, 10, 15, 16–17
  as language distinct from Standard English, 11–17
  names for, 3–4, 17n2, 17n3
  nonstandard features of, 4–7
  as slang, 7–8
African American English speech community, 3, 29
African American Language, 3, 17n3
  See also African American English
African American Literacies, 42
African American Vernacular English (AAVE), 17n2
African languages, 13, 45
  grammar, 28, 31, 32, 38, 39
  pronunciation of, 26
  vocabulary of, 20

Afrocentric curriculum, 95, 99–101, 106
Afrocentric view of African American English, 13
agreement. *See* subject-verb agreement
ain't, 36
Ajirotutu, Cheryl, 100
Ali, Muhammad, 15, 49
Alim, H. Samy, 41
alliteration, 45–46, 118, 119
alternative rhetorics, 103, 106–7
American Association for Applied Linguistics, 89
American Tongues, 90
antithesis, 118
Appalachian English, 10, 86, 91
  See also Southern White speech
a- prefix, 91
Asante, Molefi Kete, 42, 95
ashy, 23
aspect, 31, 32–34
assignments, 76, 121–25
  audiolingual, 84–85
  contrastive analysis, 84
  in culturally appropriate teaching, 96–98
  on dialect awareness, 91
  freewriting, 104
  grammar exercises, 81
attitude
  toward African American English, *see* language attitudes
  toward writing, 100
audiolingual pattern practice, 84–85, 87, 88

culturally appropriate teaching
(CAT), 94–102, 107–8
assignments, 124–25
current traditional rhetoric, 75
cut your eyes, 7

Dalji, Hafeezah AdamaDavia, 99
Dandy, Evelyn, 27, 30, 35, 79
Daniels, Harvey, 69, 82, 88
deep, 23
deep structure, 9–10, 14
def, 7
Dekalb County (Georgia) school
district, 87
Delpit, Lisa, 80, 81
demographics, of African
American English users, 29
derivation, of African American
English, 6
Deutsch, Martin, 59
dialect
African American English as,
8–11, 10, 15, 16–17
Standard American English as,
8
dialect awareness approach, 89–
94, 107–8
assignments, 122–24
dialect interference, 61–63, 71n2,
75, 83
*A Dictionary of Linguistics and
Phonetics,* 11
directness, 42, 45, 118
discourse strategies, 42–48
DISTAR Language program, 75,
80
done, 33, 34
dope, 23
double negative, 36
double subject, 38–39, 40
double verb, 39, 40
Douglass, Frederick, 51, 96
Dozens, 43, 45
Drumgoold, 96
Dunbar, Paul Laurence, 5

Ebonics, 3, 17n3
See also African American
English
-ed, missing, 31, 32, 33, 62, 101,
117
Elbow, Peter, 103, 106
elocution movement, 61
-en, missing, 33
English as a Second Dialect
(ESD), 82–89, 107–8
assignments, 122
English as a Second Language
(ESL), 16, 83
See also second language
learning
enslaved Africans, 10–11, 12, 14,
44, 58, 96
See also specific names
Equiano, Olaudah, 96
eradicationists, 55, 57–58
error analysis, 85, 88–89
error marking, 81, 105
Errors and Expectations, 70
Ethiopian alphabet, 97
Eurocentric view, 10–11
Evans, Henry, 103
exaggerated language, 48

Farr, Marcia. *See* Whiteman,
Marcia Farr
Farrell, Thomas, 59
Feigenbaum, Irwin, 82
field dependence, 43, 51n2, 104,
119
finna, 32
Flower, Linda, 66
folk stories, 47
assignments involving, 97–98
Fox, Thomas, 95, 96
freewriting, 104
Freire, Paulo, 95
fresh, 23
fused constructions, 36, 37–41
future *be,* 9
future tense, 32

Authors

Teresa M. Redd earned her PhD in education from the University of Maryland, College Park, where she specialized in composition and linguistics. For twenty years, she taught in Howard University's English department, whose faculty and students inspired her to publish the composition textbook *Revelations: An Anthology of Expository Essays by and about Blacks*. For ten of those years, she also directed the Writing Across the Curriculum Program for the College of Arts & Sciences. Although she continues to direct the program, in August 2003 she became the first director of Howard's Center for Excellence in Teaching, Learning, and Assessment.

Karen Schuster Webb holds a PhD from Indiana University's Program in TESOL and Applied Linguistics, and she is a co-author of *Speaking & Writing: A Communications Guide for the Professional*. Having served on the faculty at both Indiana and Howard University, she chaired the language education program at the University of Kentucky and soon afterward became dean of the College of Education at Southern University, Baton Rouge. Currently, she is founding dean of the Graduate School of Education at Alliant International University.

This book was typeset in Sabon by Electronic Imaging.
The typeface used on the cover was ZaphEllipt BT.
The book was printed on 60-lb. Accent Opaque paper by Versa Press, Inc.